SHADE GARDENING

SHADE GARDENING

Series Concept: Robert J. Dolezal
Encyclopedia Concept: Barbara K. Dolezal
Managing Editor: Louise Damberg
Copy Editors: Nancy Strege, Kathy Talley-Jones
Photography Editor: John M. Rickard
Designer: Jerry Simon
Layout Artists: Rik Boyd, Andrea Reider
Photoshop Artist: Ryan Pressler
Horticulturists: Carrie Heinley, Peggy Henry, Kathy Talley-Jones
Photo Stylists: Joyce M. Almstad, Carrie Heinley, Peggy Henry
Research: Dave Bullis, Shelley Ring Diamond
Index: Rick Hurd

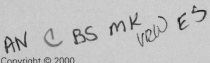

Copyright © 2000
Creative Publishing international, Inc.
5900 Green Oak Drive
Minnetonka, MN 55343
1-800-328-3895
All rights reserved
Printed in U.S.A. by World Color Press
10 9 8 7 6 5 4 3 2 1

President/CEO: David D. Murphy
Vice President/Editorial: Patricia K. Jacobsen
Vice President/Retail Sales & Marketing: Richard M. Miller

Home Improvement/*Gardening*
Executive Editor: Bryan Trandem
Editorial Director: Jerri Farris
Creative Director: Tim Himsel

Created by: Dolezal & Associates,
in partnership with Creative Publishing international, Inc.,
in cooperation with Black & Decker.
BLACK&DECKER is a trademark of the Black & Decker
Corporation and is used under license.

Library of Congress
Cataloging-in-Publication Data

(Information on file)

ISBN 0–86573–440–2 (hardcover)
ISBN 0–86573–445–3 (softcover)

PHOTOGRAPHY & ILLUSTRATION

PRINCIPAL PHOTOGRAPHY

JOHN RICKARD: pgs. *iv* (2nd from top), *v*, 3 (top), 8 (top L & top R), 9 (bot), 13 (bot), 15 (top), 16 (top), 19 (top), 20, 28 (bot), 29, 32 (top), 33, 35, 37, 38 (top), 39, 41, 42, 44 (bot), 45, 46 (step 1), 47 (step 5), 48 (bot), 50 (top), 52, 54 (bot), 57, 58 (top), 59, 60 (top), 61, 62 (top & mid), 63, 65, 68 (top & bot R), 69 (top & bot L), 72, 73 (top & mid), 74 (bot), 75 (bot steps 1–3), 76 (bot), 77, 78, 80 (top), 81 (top & mid), 87 (bot), 88 (top), 89 (bot), 90 (bot), 92 (bot), 95 (top), 98 (top & mid), 101 (bot), 103 (mid & bot), 104 (top & bot), 107 (top), 113 (top), 114 (top), 115 (mid & bot)

OTHER PHOTOGRAPHY AND ILLUSTRATION

TIM BUTLER: pgs. *iv* (top), 4 (top L & mid R), 6 (top), 18 (bot L & R), 25 (bot), 48 (top), 66, 70, 80 (bot), 83, 84 (bot), 85 (bot), 88 (bot), 89 (mid), 90 (mid), 91 (bot), 93 (mid), 94 (bot), 96 (top), 99 (top), 103 (top), 104 (mid), 105, 106 (mid), 107 (bot), 109 (mid & bot), 111 (bot)

KYLE CHESSER: pgs. *iv* (3rd from top), *vii*, 17, 18 (top L & R), 19 (mid), 21, 40, 44 (top), 53 (step 3), 54 (top), 55, 62 (bot), 73 (bot), 74 (top), 75 (top steps 1–2)

CREATIVE PUBLISHING INTERNATIONAL: pgs. 3 (bot L), 12 (bot), 56 (bot), 68 (bot L), 69 (bot R), 76 (top), 86, 95 (mid), 114 (bot)

CORBIS/WOLFGANG KAEHLER: pg. 5 (bot)

DOUG DEALEY: pgs. 9 (top), 13 (top), 15 (bot), 24, 38 (bot), 56 (top), 87 (top)

REED ESTABROOK: pgs. *iv* (bot), *vi*, *viii*, 2, 4 (bot), 14 (top), 22, 28 (top), 36 (bot), 58 (bot), 96 (bot), 101 (top), 106 (bot)

DAVID GOLDBERG: pgs. 25 (top), 34, 64

SAXON HOLT: pgs. 50 (bot), 51, 84 (top), 85 (top), 90 (top), 92 (top), 93 (top & bot), 94 (top & mid), 96 (mid), 97 (top), 98 (bot), 99 (bot), 100 (mid), 108, 109 (top), 110 (top), 111 (top & mid), 112, 115 (top)

IMAGEPOINT: pgs. 5 (top), 8 (bot), 16 (bot), 19 (bot), 30, 36 (top), 46 (step 2), 47 (steps 3, 4, 6), 49, 53 (steps 1–2), 60 (bot), 82, 88 (mid), 89 (top)

PHOTODISC IMAGE STOCK: pg. 12 (top)

CHARLES SLAY: pgs. 6 (mid & bot), 10, 81 (bot), 87 (mid), 97 (mid & bot), 99 (mid), 100 (top & bot), 102 (bot), 106 (top), 113 (bot)

YVONNE WILLIAMS: Cover and pgs. 3 (bot R), 7, 14 (bot), 26, 27, 32 (bot), 71, 91 (top), 95 (bot), 102 (top), 110 (bot), 113 (mid)

ILLUSTRATIONS: HILDEBRAND DESIGN

The editors acknowledge with grateful appreciation the contribution to this book of Alden Lane Nursery, Livermore, California.

SHADE
GARDENING

Author
Carol A. Crotta

Photographer
John M. Rickard

Series Concept
Robert J. Dolezal

CREATIVE
PUBLISHING
international

Minnetonka, Minnesota

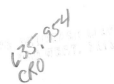

C O N T E N T S

DECORATING WITH SHADE PLANTS

Page 31

PLANTING IN SHADE

Page 43

CARING FOR SHADE PLANTS

Page 67

ENCYCLOPEDIA OF SHADE PLANTS

Page 79

PLANT HARDINESS

Page 117

INTRODUCTION

*W*hen you picture a garden, it likely includes the sun shining brightly, lighting up the lawn and flower beds. Think about the garden you have savored the most, and more likely it is a cool, comfortable, shady garden nook surrounded by deep-green foliage and brilliant flowers speckled with light passing through the leaves of a nearby tree.

The shade garden, without doubt, can be the most satisfying part of any landscape.

Some gardeners worry about shade, even fear its consequences. The prospect of planning

> *Everybody needs*
> *beauty as well as bread,*
> *places to play in and pray*
> *in, where Nature may heal*
> *and cheer and give strength*
> *to body and soul alike.*
>
> JOHN MUIR

a shade garden seems difficult, and maintenance may seem harder yet, though these concerns are unnecessary. A shade garden is, after all, still a garden, with the same soil, watering, lighting, and feeding requirements as a sunny garden. The truth is, there is a wide variety of plants that not only survive shade, but positively thrive in it.

When most people think about a shade garden, they imagine only green plantings. In fact, some of the shade garden's superstars—the azaleas and impatiens, so intensely painted in the shade—would appear pallid in full sun.

There are, however, more shades of green than of any other color in the spectrum, allowing you to create a garden that is a subtly shifting sea of green plantings.

Once you've fallen in love with the shade plant array, you may want to create a shade plot of your own, which can be accomplished easily with an understanding of your soil conditions. A shade garden can be moist or dry or anywhere in between.

Indeed, it can be as beautiful and inviting as the most sun-drenched area of your yard.

S hade gardens exist in many forms. Technically, a shade garden is any garden that receives less than six hours of full sun per day, but that definition covers many common garden situations, in every part of the world, in every climate.

Perhaps a more helpful statement is this: you know a shade garden when you see one. Now look a little closer. Is the shade created by trees? Are they deciduous or evergreen? Does sunlight filter through the branches and dapple the ground below, or is there no penetration of sunlight at all?

If the shady site is created by walls or other structures, does the area ever get sun, and if so, when? Is the ambient air humid or dry? Is the shaded soil dark and moist or light and dry?

Do you live in a climate where shade is appreciated for the relief it provides from the sun's strong glare, or is your shade in a misty bower that makes it a challenge to your gardening plans?

The shade gardens shown on the following pages will help define, not limit, the range of shade gardens available to you. In fact, the specific conditions found in your garden setting should guide you in making good choices, not dictate all that you can achieve.

You can make shady areas less so by pruning trees or erecting light-colored walls or fences. Conversely, you can make sunny areas more shaded by planting trees or building structural overhangs. If your soil is too moist or too dry for the plantings you desire, you can amend it. Ultimately, you can have whatever shade garden you desire with just a little planning.

> For nearly every garden and site, there's a shade garden to fulfill your desires and dreams

Made for the Shade

One of the most valued qualities of a shade garden is its ability to provide a cool, comfortable retreat from the heat of a blistering summer day.

WOODLAND GARDENS

Though a woodland garden appears to grow randomly, it is subtly structured with an overstory of trees, an understory of shrubs, and a ground level of mosses, ferns, and grasses.

Few scenes in nature are more picturesque than a woodland garden. A dense, moist woodland setting can play host to chest-deep waves of ferns and carpets of plush green and yellow moss. What a delight it is to wander through the dim, cool shade and come across a golden burst of naturalized narcissus or daffodils, a swirl of delicate lilies of the valley, where a shaft of light cutting through the branches overhead allows them to bloom. Gardeners who count woodland as part of their property—and even those who don't—can achieve this type of shade garden.

Such a natural setting can be managed to create just the perfect balance of shade and sun, trees and flowering shrubs, perennials, bulbs, and even annuals. There is a structure to the growth: the tallest trees form the overstory, or canopy; the next tallest trees and tall shrubs, the understory; regular shrubs, the shrub layer; and the lowest growing mosses, ferns, and flowers, the ground layer. Careful pruning of the over- and understories allow filtered light to fall on the shrub and ground layers, creating the best conditions for diverse planting.

If you lack a woodland setting, you can plant a miniature grove with as few as three trees. You'll also have the luxury of choosing your favorites suited to your area and planting them to allow for lower shade plantings.

In the green recesses of a shade garden, colorful flowering plants are beacons of light. Indeed, the brilliance of a color-infused shade garden easily can outshine a sunny border. The reason is contrast: while strong sun tends to drain color, deep green foliage and low light conditions intensify and energize color. Place a flowering container plant, such as magenta impatiens or purple-pink hydrangea, out in full sun. Now place it in the shade. You'll find the difference remarkable.

Some of the most color-packed flowering plants—neon-hued impatiens, electric-orange clivia, purple-pink and purple-blue hydrangeas, golden to scarlet daylilies, baby-blue forget-me-nots, multihued fuchsias and pansies—all look their finest in the shade garden and downright thrive in filtered to low light. So do shade azaleas and camellias, wisteria, foxgloves, and a host of other flowers, shrubs, vines, and ground covers. For every shade lighting condition, there are flowering plants ready to shine. Even in the deepest shade, you can create a colorful atmosphere by bringing in generally sun-loving "visitors"—flowering container plants that will tolerate shade for a time—then returning them to sunnier spots to reinvigorate.

Experimenting with color is one of the most enjoyable aspects of shade gardening. It's an exercise in optical illusion as well. Purples, blues, and blue-red tones, when massed, visually recede and add depth to a bed or border, while whites, yellows, and oranges pop right at you. You can play with depth perception and color combinations to make a strong color statement.

COLORFUL SHADE GARDENS

(Above) Most members of the lily family are stalwart additions to a shade garden, providing lush green foliage and a variety of colors.

(Left) The subtle colors of these shade-loving flowers would wash out in full sunlight, but they emerge in shade.

(Right) The color of hydrangea, whether purple-pink or purple-blue, is determined by the acidity or alkalinity of your soil as much as by the variety you plant.

FOLIAGE IN A SHADE GARDEN

Imagine a garden composed solely of plants that have been chosen for their foliage. When you leave flowers out of the equation, you begin to see the garden and its possibilities in a different way. The shapes of the plants, the textures of their leaves, and the nuances of their shadings come into clear and intriguing focus. Foliage may take a backseat in a sunny border, but in a shade garden, greenery and unusual leaves can stand front and center.

A great number of plants that are grown for their interesting, unusual, and sometimes very colorful foliage thrive in shady conditions. If you want the lushest and coolest shade landscape imaginable, plant a palette of greens. Professional colorists will tell you that there are more shades of green than of any other color. Green is a cool color, and green foliage enhances what we like best about shade—its soothing and restful quality.

If you decide to design a shade garden using only greens, your possibilities are vast. You can work within one plant family, for example, hosta [see Encyclopedia of Shade Plants, pg. 79], which is prized for its variety of plant size, leaf shape and texture, and shadings—ranging from chartreuse to deep green.

If you are partial to color, consider the foliage plants that cloak themselves with brilliant hues rivaling those of the most vivid flowers. Coleus, for example, comes in an electrifying palette ranging from acid yellow to deep burgundy, with greens, oranges, maroons, and bright pinks in between. The ground cover commonly known as the chameleon plant features heart-shaped leaves splashed with cream, pink, and red—and no two of them are alike.

(Above) Besides its uniquely shaped dark-green foliage, holly also provides a burst of color in winter with its colorful berries.

(Right) Coleus is just one of many foliage plants that cloak themselves in a brilliant palette of color.

Some of the hosta group include varieties that feature cream, yellow, or chartreuse edgings and variegated swirls. Shade foliage plants can be used in tandem with flowering plants, either to contrast with or echo the flower's hue. For contrast, plant one of the many coleus varieties. For a complementary effect, mass similarly colored flowers with your shade plantings.

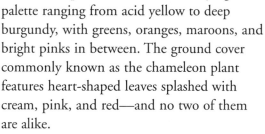

(Left) The deeply dentated and fine-cut foliage of Japanese maple, Acer palmatum, *turns a brilliant red in autumn, but some cultivars, such as 'Bloodgood,' sport red-tinged leaves all season long.*

When you think of a desert garden, you likely think of cactus, shrubs, and succulents basking under a blistering hot sun. Truth be known, desert plants can benefit from some shade, at least during the hottest part of the day, especially in regions where hot means really, really hot. Too much sun can scorch even the most heat-tolerant plants, bleaching out their color, giving them a bad case of sunburn in spots, and finally scarring them.

If you'd like to plant a desert garden in existing shade, it will work best if the area receives sun for about half the day, particularly in the morning. Succulents such as kalanchoes, sedums, and Christmas cactus especially need some relief from the sun. Cactus and succulents planted in the shade will be greener and more lush—they even may spread out to reach for available sun. The one downside is that they generally will flower less in shade than in sun.

Desert plants in the shade need even less water than their usual sparse requirements and can develop fungal disease if they get too much, since shaded soil tends to hold in moisture. If the soil is dry more than 1–2 inches (25–50 mm) beneath the surface, it's time to water. If you are planting in beds, you may want to consider using a raised bed, which will improve drainage. Desert plants tend to like a sandy potting mix of one-half compost and one-half pumice, perlite, or volcanic rock that is ⅛–¼ inch (3–6 mm) in diameter. You also want to fertilize a little less in shade. Low-nitrogen liquid fertilizers and fish emulsion work well, but use them at one-quarter strength every watering.

If you don't have shade but would like to create it, consider building an arbor or lath house, an open structure with wood laths spaced at regular intervals across the roof [see Constructing a Shade Arbor, pg. 25]. Such structures provide filtered shade that can protect your desert plantings from the hot summer sun.

DESERT SHADE GARDENS

Though most people think of cactus and succulents as sun lovers, some shade is necessary to prevent them from scorching or becoming sunburned, especially when planted in containers.

The variation in shading and shadowing created by the architecture of this traditional New Mexican veranda allows a wide range of partial-shade lovers to prosper in its inviting central courtyard.

MOIST SHADE GARDENS

There's a good chance, as you plan your shade garden, that the image you have in mind is that of a moist shade garden, probably because shaded areas are damp in many cases. Where there is little sun, there is little moisture evaporation.

Moist shade isn't confined to woodland settings. It can occur in areas of open shade created by tall buildings, along fences and walls, and under patio covers. Moist shade is a gracious host to many shade-loving plants and shrubs, such as hydrangeas and azaleas, most mosses and ferns, impatiens, phlox, and primroses, to name just a few. When planted in rich, loose soil, a moist shade garden can enjoy great success and add a splendid touch of coolness to your yard in summer.

If these are the plantings you crave, realize that it is easy to revamp dry shade areas by installing an in-ground irrigation system [see Installing an In-ground Irrigation System, pg. 35]. A number of today's home irrigation systems provide multiple options for getting water to your plot—but you will need to be vigilant with your watering regimen. Too much water will cause many moist-shade plants, such as impatiens and most bulbs, to develop fungal disease. Adding pachysandra or bugleweed to the mix will help retain moisture. In addition, you'll need to monitor moist garden areas for poor air circulation, which can go hand in hand with shady corners of a yard—particularly if the yard slopes downward. Clearing away low-growing shrub and tree branches will go a long way toward improving air flow.

Moisture lovers include water lilies (top), which rely on the oxygen in water to thrive, and orchids (above), which may require regular misting to maintain the high humidity level they crave.

The humidity provided by a garden fountain creates a perfect environment for these moisture-loving shade plants.

ry shade areas are as conducive to planting as moist ones. Dry shade can be created by certain trees and shrubs, especially shallow-rooted and heavy feeders such as conifers, beeches, and Norway maples, which can suck moisture out of the ground and away from tender-rooted perennials and annuals. Dry shade also can be created by wide-roof eaves and patio-cover extensions that block rain from reaching the ground. In addition, dry shade can be created in areas where the soil drains too quickly or the ambient air is hot.

DRY SHADE GARDENS

You can correct for this condition by deep digging and incorporating large doses of amendments, or by using raised beds with drip irrigation systems or overhead misters that mount on trees and create humidity. The best solution always is to adapt your plantings to suit the site. Not all shade-loving plants need constant heavy moisture to thrive. Certain of the epimediums, particularly *E.* × *perralchicum* 'Frohnleiten,' tolerate dryness, as do the ground covers barren strawberry, lunaria, lilyturf, Asian wood poppy, ribbon grass, spotted dead nettle, vinca minor (periwinkle), aspidistra, and sweet alyssum, among many others.

All dry shade plantings can benefit from some soil amendment with a moisture-retentive material such as peat moss, leaf mold, or mushroom compost. If the dryness is caused by shallow-rooted trees and shrubs, you might add a slow-release nitrogen fertilizer to the amendments to help satisfy hungry roots. After planting, place a layer of mulch over the soil surface to hold in the moisture and help reduce the rate of evaporation.

(Above) Many ground covers, such as bacopa, do not require heavy watering or even constant moisture to thrive.

(Left) Vining ground covers, such as vinca, spread to find the light and moisture they need.

SHADE GARDENS IN FILTERED LIGHT

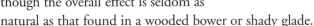

In the world of shade gardens, filtered light is as close to perfection as it gets. No doubt you've seen and appreciated this type of light—the beautiful dappled effect of sunlight filtering through shifting leaves and branches overhead to speckle the plants below. Filtered light typically occurs when there is a high canopy of trees, but it also can be created with trellising or shade cloth, though the overall effect is seldom as natural as that found in a wooded bower or shady glade.

Filtered light differs from part, partial, and half shade, all of which occur due to a lack of direct sun on an area for part of the day. How much sun the area receives, and when, also makes a difference. Shade plants will do fine if the full sun hits early in the morning and ends before noon. If the full sun arrives around midday and lasts through the afternoon, however, sun-loving plants are a better option, or you can choose plants that tolerate both sun and some shade.

With filtered shade, as the sunlight shifts and dances across the plants below the canopy, the filtered light offers all the benefits of the sun's direct light without the intense heat that can toast plants.

If you have a filtered-light situation, you know how blessed you are. A great variety of shade plants will grow in filtered light, and even some sun lovers, such as flowering tobacco and daylilies, will be happy in spots with strong filtered light. In fact, in strong-sun areas, almost all but the toughest flowering plants are happier with some filtered sun during the hottest part of the day.

Before planting in a filtered-light area, "map" the sections that receive the strongest and steadiest light by sprinkling sand to mark them. Plant varieties that tolerate the greatest amount of sun in these spots to avoid scorching more delicate shade plants.

(Top right) The filtered light created by a tree canopy provides a perfect environment for this vine-covered fence—and (above) an angelic environment for a ground cover.

Flowering shade lovers are encouraged to bloom by the dappled light provided from the delicate overstory of a tree.

Variety is the spice of life, particularly in a garden. A great way to add new flavor to your shade garden is to place some of your shade lovers in decorative containers or pots and set them at interesting points among your in-ground perennial and shrub plantings. The type of pot—rustic wood, classic terra cotta or stone, oriental enameled, even a hollowed-out tree stump or log—can enhance the atmosphere of your garden while helping you establish a theme.

SHADE PLANTS IN CONTAINERS

For a week or so, maintain the plants in their original plastic nursery pots while you experiment with different arrangements. Once you hit on one you like, leave the plants where they are for a few more days to make sure they adjust to light conditions in that area.

Many shade-loving plants do well in containers. Camellias and azaleas, for example, can be happy for some years in pots if they are fed with cottonseed meal at two-month intervals after their blooming season. Heavenly bamboo also does well in pots, offering both colorful stems and berries. Fuchsias, particularly trailing fuchsias placed in hanging baskets lined with sheets of sphagnum moss, thrive in light to medium shade. They are another good container candidate. Shade annuals, ferns, and small perennials such as primroses also make fine container plantings.

You can fill a container with a variety of trailing and upright plants or simply spotlight a single show stopper— an elegant fern or tall fuchsia. Regardless of which plants you choose, you'll find that you will water containers in shade gardens less than you would those set in sun, since evaporation is less of a problem. Choosing plants with similar watering requirements will make your job that much easier as well.

Shade-loving plants in containers offer the added benefit of reduced watering requirements.

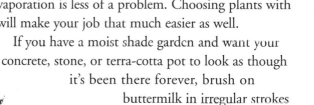

If you have a moist shade garden and want your concrete, stone, or terra-cotta pot to look as though it's been there forever, brush on buttermilk in irregular strokes and rub fresh moss across the surface. If you keep the exterior of the pot moist over the next few weeks, moss will gradually develop on the surface, adding an aged, green-patina look to the container.

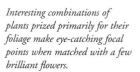

Interesting combinations of plants prized primarily for their foliage make eye-catching focal points when matched with a few brilliant flowers.

W hen embarking on any gardening project, the best place to begin is by asking yourself—and ultimately your nursery or garden center professional—a series of questions. While it's less fun than getting your hands dirty, it can save you hours of unnecessary labor and ensure a successful outcome.

To begin, think about where your shade garden is located, both geographically and within your environs. Next, think about the type of shade garden you'd like to have and the purpose you want it to serve in your yard as a whole. Consider what types of plants will suit your situation and purpose, and how their shapes and sizes will blend with or highlight existing buildings and other outdoor structures.

You'll need to evaluate your planting site to determine if it needs alterations to make it more amenable to shade gardening. That evaluation will include studying your soil and finding out what amendments may be required for the plantings you desire. Once you know this, you should acquire the proper tools, equipment, and other materials, such as fertilizers and irrigation systems, required to create and maintain your garden. Last but not least, you'll want to know the best sources for acquiring plants, tools, materials, and mulch.

As you go through the following questions, keep a pad of paper handy. Some answers will come easily, others will require a bit of investigation or thought. When you can answer them all, you'll be ready to put your plan into action.

Even seasoned gardeners will rediscover the importance of this exercise, because shade and soil conditions can change from season to season, not only with the growth of their own shade-producing shrubs and trees but also their neighbors'.

Evaluating your shady location is the first and most important step in planning a shade garden

A Garden Checklist

This rustic backyard entry would appear less inviting without its colorful shade bed; instead, the feeling is serene and welcoming.

CHOOSING A SITE

Where is your shade garden located? While "in my yard" is a tempting response, it won't take you very far. "Where?" is a critical question, meant to address everything from the big picture to the smallest detail.

The dappled light this area receives makes it not only perfect for shade plantings but for people seeking a cool retreat.

For starters, where, geographically, do you live? Climate greatly determines the types of plants that will grow successfully in your area and the type of preparation and care they will need. The United States Department of Agriculture (USDA) publishes a map dividing North America into eleven plant "hardiness" zones, based on the average annual minimum temperature each experiences. Every zone features a range of temperatures that will guide you in choosing your plants, shrubs, and trees [see USDA Plant Hardiness Map, pg. 116]. The Encyclopedia of Shade Plants [see pg. 79] will tell you which hardiness zones support the plants you may be considering. With both resources, you'll be able to choose plants that have a high chance of success.

Now, about your yard. Is your proposed shade garden defined by trees and shrubs, or does the shade come from adjacent tall city buildings? Does the area have filtered light, shade only part of the day, or dense shade? How do these conditions change with the progression of the day and seasons?

Will your shade garden be near your home or another structure? If so, do you want to accentuate and enhance—or basically hide—the style or color of the structure? Does the area get hit by wind, or do you live in the mountains, where the air is thin? If so, maintaining adequate moisture will be an issue. Are you near an ocean? Coast air from large bodies of water moderates temperature, but ocean air tends to be salty, which can limit the types of plants you can grow successfully.

Understanding your shade garden's location will define and refine your options.

A lattice-roofed arbor provides perfect dappled light for creating any shade garden you desire.

Planting in the shade differs from planting a shade garden. A shade garden usually is designed to serve a purpose. Do you desire an effect—a romantic retreat; a serene Oriental garden of mosses, rocks, and bamboo; a springtime extravaganza of azaleas and dogwoods all in bloom; a summer spectacle of brilliant impatiens or coleus?

With a shade garden, you can have it all, from bright to muted colors, from multiple hues to a single-color theme. You also can achieve a shifting sea of greens with few flowers by planting an all-foliage shade garden. Create drama with planted urns and statuary or simple comfort with a macramé hammock under some tall trees over a shade lawn.

You may want your shade garden to serve a practical purpose—the main function being that it is low maintenance. Do you have a great expanse of shady area but little time to tend it? Consider a shade ground cover such as pachysandra or ribbon grass, punctuated with plantings of a few larger perennials.

Does your yard need a cool eating area? You might want to create a shady dining room under a big tree or cluster of trees on a carpet of ground cover, surrounded by walls of shade plants.

You may want only to add some structure and visual interest to a woodland that forms part of your property. This is a perfect place to try out some non-native plants alongside those common to your region.

Do you want a formal garden that suits your shaded city lot, or do you want a more natural look?

Finally, you may just want to reclaim unused areas of the yard—back corners under heavy trees and borders under deep roof eaves—that you've been reluctant or unwilling to take on in the past.

Knowing the purpose of your shade garden will give you a blueprint for your gardening project, helping to focus your efforts for greatest success.

SHADE GARDENS FOR EVERY PURPOSE

A slatted screen provides privacy and a perfect spot to display shade-loving container plants.

Since color is kept to a minimum in traditional Japanese gardens, they often offer inspirational combinations of plants with contrasting shapes, forms, and foliage.

PLANT SHAPE AND FORM

Gardens get much of their personality from the interplay of plant sizes, colors, and textures, as well as from plant shapes. A mix of shapes—tall and skinny, round and squat, low and rangy, short and compact—can be used to great effect. Repetitive use of a plant shape, such as the mound, also can make for an interesting design, particularly if it either mimics the planting bed's shape or contrasts with it. Your choice of plant shape can mirror the architecture of your home or other outdoor structures, emphasize hardscaping, and even compensate for overly wide or narrow lots.

Is your yard wide and wandering? A centrally placed bed, planted pyramid style with low to tall plants at the midpoint, can pull a yard together visually and give it a focal point. Would you like to accentuate the width of your yard? A series of low mounding shrubs or plants set in curved beds across the width of the yard can achieve this. Would you like to echo the tall buildings surrounding your city garden? Tall, spirelike cypress will lead the eye upward. A formal French-style house calls for manicured plants—in fact, the more formal the architecture, the more clean the shape of the foundation plantings should be. Other architectural styles—English cottage and Spanish hacienda, for example—lend themselves to a softer, wilder style of planting; rangy, billowing plants will do well in such settings. If your house lacks a distinct style, the plantings can help create one, allowing you to be playful with plant forms. A small house can get a tongue-in-cheek touch from a planting of giant sunflowers that seem to dwarf it. A fifties-style box in a Southern clime can take on a South Seas touch with a planting of tropical "forest" around it. Whichever plant shapes you choose, keep in mind their appearance once the plants reach maturity.

(Top) Of the shade plants renowned for their shape and form, hostas reign supreme. (Left) Combining different textures and forms lends visual interest and unique personality to a shade garden.

Before you gather any greengoods, analyze your site thoroughly and determine the changes and alterations necessary to create an attractive shade environment. First, consider the light. Does a too-full tree let in less light than you'd like? Consider pruning the tree to allow more light to penetrate [see Pruning Deciduous Trees, pg. 27]. Could the area benefit from reflected light? Think about painting structures light colors or adding light-colored pebbles to adjacent areas.

Next, think about your soil as well as the soil properties required by your preferred plants. For example, do you intend to plant among the exposed roots of an old tree? If the soil is just too dry and compacted, consider constructing a raised bed around the tree about 6 feet (1.8 m) from the base of the trunk. A raised bed also is appropriate if your soil is alkaline and the plants you want call for acid conditions, or vice versa. Testing your soil [see Performing a Soil Test, pg. 41] will help you determine its pH level. Most shade-loving plants prefer a loose, humus-rich soil that holds some moisture but drains well. Is the soil not loose enough? Leaf mold or organic compost can help lighten it. So can peat moss, which also will acidify the soil. Is the soil too acid? Adding limestone or crushed oyster shells can help neutralize it.

Before you plant, you also need to evaluate moisture levels in the ground and in the air. Does your planting area drain very slowly after a rain or watering, or is the ground too dry? Consider an irrigation system, such as a slow-release drip system [see A Simple Drip System, pg. 37]. Is the air dry, or does wind tend to whip through the area on a regular basis? Overhead misters can help add humidity. Is the area damp and dank? Poor air circulation can be a significant problem for shade gardens, fostering mold and mildew and generally inhibiting plant growth. Thinning out existing plantings and pruning up shrubs can help alleviate this problem.

ADAPTING THE SITE

Since the structure of the understory is a critical design element in shade gardens, it can be exposed beautifully through the use of artificial lighting.

A trickling fountain provides a decorative element as well as a ready water source for a container shade garden.

CHOOSING PLANTS

Your plans are complete and the ground is ready. Now you begin perhaps the most enjoyable part of your project—shopping for plants. With all the choices available, at your local retail stores, in the electronic marketplace, and through the mail, the array can be intimidating. Use the climate, soil, light, and moisture requirements of your shady plot as your guide.

Let's say you're at your garden center or nursery, and your eye chances upon a lovely flowering plant you'd really like to have. It probably is hardy for your climate zone, but check the Encyclopedia of Shade Plants [see pg. 79] to be certain about its climate needs. Next, check the light requirements on the plant tag and in the encyclopedia. For instance, the tag and encyclopedia concur that the plant requires partial shade, meaning it can tolerate some direct sun for a portion of the day, and you also discover that it prefers a moist environment, with a slightly alkaline pH soil.

(Right) In addition to checking that flowers and foliage are free of obvious disease, any signs of pest infestation, and that the plant is not rootbound, look at the plant tag to determine its sun requirements.

After checking the conditions in your garden, you find out that it's a perfect match. Now you need to check the plant's health. Does it seem hardy, with new growth at the base? Are there any yellow or brown leaves, spotted leaves, or leaves that look as though they've been chewed?

Turn the pot on its side and examine its roots. Are they growing out of the drain? Gently slide the plant free of the pot. Do the roots seem thick, crowded, and knotted together at the bottom of the rootball? If so, the plant has been in the pot too long and is likely rootbound, which ultimately will stunt its growth. Purchase a younger specimen with correct root development instead of trying to resurrect a plant that's well past its prime.

Checking out plants in this manner before you invest in them will save you time, money, and later disappointment.

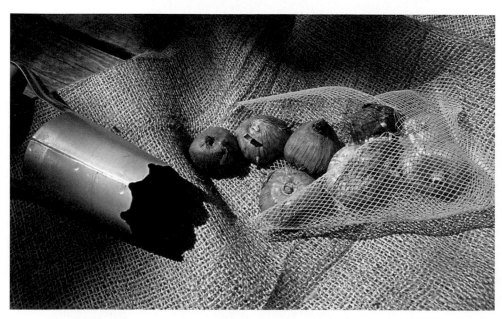

Bulbs should be firm, uniform in shape, and show no signs of sprouting growth.

The greatest factor in a shade plant's ability to survive and thrive is the soil that surrounds its roots. A plant draws all the nutrients it cannot produce itself from soil. While some plants are more tolerant than others of their soil, many have marked preferences and needs that, if not met, will result in poor growth or even failure.

ASSESSING SOIL CONDITIONS

Evaluating your soil is a three-part inquiry. To start, you need to know its current composition. Is it loose, or hard, compacted clay? Does it drain too quickly and stay very dry most of the time, or does it drain slowly and remain boggy? In all of these cases, you likely need to add amendments. Most shade plants relish a loose, well-drained, humus-rich, consistently moist, loamy soil that mimics a woodland floor. Others, however, prefer light, dry soil, while still others need the type of drippy wet soil found along ponds and stream beds. Shade plants also generally prefer either an acidic or neutral soil. To determine the pH level of your soil, test different points in the garden area [see Preparing to Plant, pg. 40] so you can properly amend for your chosen plantings.

Your second inquiry regards the soil requirements of these plants. Do they need light loam; prefer acid, neutral, or alkaline soil; or require a moist or dry soil? You will find these answers in the Encyclopedia of Shade Plants [see pg. 79]; also make sure you check the plant tag for the grower's recommendations.

Once you've determined the soil you have, your last inquiry regards the types of amendments you'll need to go from the soil you have to the soil you want. Working in well-rotted manure, leaf mold, and organic compost helps lighten dense, compacted soil and aids moisture retention in sandy, dry, quick-draining soil. Incorporating polymers—crystals that soak up water and expand to many times their original size, acting as mini-reservoirs for thirsty roots—also can help with moisture retention. If you need to acidify your soil, work in peat moss and leaf mold and supplement with monthly or bimonthly doses of a water-soluble acid fertilizer.

The final and most important inquiry regards the soil compatibility of the plants you'd like to have. If they have different soil needs, you still can have them in the same garden by planting in raised beds or containers filled with the proper soil.

For many shade plants, the soil mix called "loam"—equal parts clay, sand, and silt—is an ideal planting medium.

TOOLS AND MATERIALS

Your shade-garden shopping list may extend beyond plants and soil amendments. What tools and materials do you need to get the job done?

A set of basic garden tools—a hand and full-size spade, shovel, rake, and cultivators—is essential. If you want to create shade, you might want to pick up some prefabricated trelliswork panels and lengths of shade cloth.

Unless you live in a continually wet climate, you'll need a watering can equipped with a variety of heads for heavy to fine spray patterns, for established and tender young plants.

Fertilizers are necessary to sustain a healthy, thriving shade garden. There are dry fertilizers, liquid fertilizers that contain varying percentages of the essential elements—nitrogen, phosphorus, and potassium—inorganic fertilizers, which are produced chemically in laboratories, and organics, which tend to release their nutrients more slowly over time. To wend your way through this bewildering array of choices, read package labels carefully.

Insect and disease controls also are widely available, but better left for the time when you perceive a particular need. You also might want to consider buying B-1 liquid fertilizer, which many believe, when applied just after transplanting, helps ease transplant shock and, for dry soil, polymer water-retention crystals, which absorb many times their weight in water and act as reservoirs for thirsty plants.

(Above and top) Fertilizers and most pesticides are available in a range of media—from liquid to dry forms, in either organic or inorganic formulations. Always follow label instructions to the letter for best results.

(Right) Plant supports come in a variety of shapes, materials, and sizes, lending staking as well as good air circulation to growing plants. (Far right) A range of hand and hose irrigation tools allows the gardener to direct water precisely where it's needed.

Some of the best resources for planting advice are your local nurseries and home or garden stores. They usually are staffed with professionals who understand the specifics of your area's soil, climate, and regional conditions and stock plants best suited to it.

The first question you should ask the garden center experts is if they actually garden. Do they know the soil requirements, recommended amendments and fertilizers, watering and feeding requirements, susceptibility to pests and diseases, and ultimate height and width of your desired plantings? If you find someone who does, latch on to that person and cultivate, so to speak, that relationship. It will be invaluable to you for years of gardening to come.

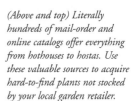

Apart from local resources, you can take advantage of the many catalogs available, both by mail order or in the electronic marketplace. Many specialize in rare plants—old roses, heritage vegetables, iris of all types. Some, but not all, have knowledgeable folk at the end of a toll-free number. There also are many associations—often called "societies"—devoted to one plant or another that publish newsletters chronicling breakthrough breeding and cultivation techniques. The one cautionary note about all of these resources is that results are seldom uniform in all locations. Pay attention to the plant hardiness zones [see USDA Plant Hardiness Zones, pg. 79] and buy only if plants meet your climate and shade requirements.

(Above and top) Literally hundreds of mail-order and online catalogs offer everything from hothouses to hostas. Use these valuable sources to acquire hard-to-find plants not stocked by your local garden retailer.

Your local garden retailer is the most reliable source for plants indigenous to your area; for more exotic or non-native species, choose seeds as another option, or visit a local arboretum.

SHADE GARDENING PLANNING FLOWCHART

Aflowchart is a written checklist that allows you to quickly scan the major decisions that should be reviewed as you consider a garden project. The one illustrated here specifically deals with the decisions gardeners must make when they undertake planting in shady locations. A few minutes spent with the checklist will ensure you remember each waypoint to a successful project. Refer to the checklist before beginning a new project—it will save you time and effort, including second trips to the nursery or garden store.

1 Site Choice Questions:
Where is your garden located, both geographically and within your environs? Is your proposed shade garden defined by trees and shrubs, or does the shade come from adjacent tall city buildings? Does it have filtered light, shade only part of the day, or dense shade? Will your shade garden be near your home or another structure? If so, do you want to accentuate or basically hide the style or color of the structure? Is the air thin or is the site exposed to wind or near an ocean or other body of water?

DETERMINING YOUR OBJECTIVES

2 Goal Questions:
What type of shade garden would you like to have and what purpose do you want it to serve in your yard as a whole? Do you desire an effect—a romantic retreat, a serene space, or a display of brilliant color? Are you seeking to complement or contrast with the style of your house through your plantings? Do you want a more formal or more natural look? When do you want the project finished? How much ongoing care will the garden require?

ALLOCATING TIME AND SCHEDULING

3 Scale Questions:
Is your space wide and wandering? Do you want to accentuate the dimensions of your space, or diminish them? Would you like to echo the tall buildings surrounding your city garden? How much time will planning and designing require? Will your project require special equipment or materials? How much time will it take, and will you need any assistance to complete it successfully?

PLANNING FOR THE PROJECT

4 **Plant Selection Questions:**
What are the growth habits, care needs, and color display features of the plants you desire? Does your planned space provide for those requirements? Does the site receive partial sun, and if so, is it in early morning, midday, or late afternoon? In the garden store, are the greengoods well maintained, healthy, and free of pests? How wide is the selection, and are plants of appropriate size available when you need them? Do the plantings seem hardy, with new growth at the base? Are there any yellow or brown leaves, spotted leaves, or leaves that look as though they've been chewed? Are the roots of the plants you intend to buy growing out of the bottom drainage holes of the pot? Is the garden store staff knowledgeable and helpful?

PREPARING TO PURCHASE SHADE PLANTS

SOIL PREPARATION, MATERIALS, AND TOOLS

5 **Preparation Questions:**
What is the quality of your soil? Is it loose or hard, compacted clay? Does it drain too quickly and stay very dry most of the time, or does it drain slowly and stay boggy? Do you know your soil's pH level, or do you need to test it or have it tested? What materials, supplies, tools, and amendments will you require? What fertilizers are needed for the plants you have chosen? Will your shade garden require any special type of irrigation system? To which kinds of pests and diseases are your desired plantings prone, and what type of preventive measures might you need to employ?

FINDING HELP AND INFORMATION

6 **Resource and Aid Questions:**
Where will you turn for expert advice? Do you have current catalogs, periodicals, and books containing information about the plants and garden techniques you will require? Does your garden retailer have knowledgeable staff able to assist your decisions and answer your questions? Have you identified your USDA plant hardiness zone and microclimate? Are you familiar with online electronic resources, or do you have access to your agricultural extension office agent? Are there gardening classes available though local educators? Are there local experts that broadcast in radio or television media to whom you may turn with questions?

The most critical step in the shade gardening process is exactly what you may think: evaluating your site. Not all shade situations are alike, nor are shady areas within the same garden equal. The differences are easy to see, and you will want to note them because they will determine what plants you buy and their soil and watering requirements.

In this chapter, you will find out how to evaluate your shady location, from assessing the quality and quantity of the sunlight (or the absence thereof) to analyzing its prevailing soil conditions and potential as a home for your plants.

Hand in hand with knowing your site's conditions is considering the function of your intended shady garden—a showcase for shade-loving flowers and foliage, a tranquil retreat for quiet reading or napping, a conversation corner or dining area. While the trees, fences, buildings, and other structures that create your shady plot will influence the shape and plant content of your garden, the purpose it serves is fully up to you.

Finally, depending on your circumstances, you may want to know how to increase light in your shady location—or how to create shade in a sunny one. To accomplish either or both goals, we offer tips and complete step-by-step instructions on pruning to let in light and constructing a shade cover to protect plantings from the effects of too much sun.

> **Understanding your site and how to adapt it to your needs is the first step toward shade garden success**

Preparing to Plant

One of the great visual joys of a shade garden is how colors are intensified when cast against a background of deep-green foliage.

EVALUATING A SHADE LOCATION

The first order of business is to take a hard look at your garden—and not just once. Take five or six trips into the yard starting in early morning, then late morning, noon, and at two and four o'clock in the afternoon. Make a note of how much sun each area of the yard gets at each time. Repeat this process at several points during the year, during different seasons, as the sun appears to rise to different angles in the sky.

Next, characterize the type of light each area of the yard receives. This, too, will change as the day goes on. Does an area receive limited light all day, or full sun part of the day and little the rest? If the latter is true, you have partial, or half shade. Does an area receive dappled shade, that is, shade created by sunlight filtering through tree branches, speckling the plants below? That's moderate shade. Finally, if your area is shaded but remains bright all day, you have hit nirvana—light shade. Though there are plantings that will thrive in any of these conditions, light shade will give you the largest choice of plants.

The next step in evaluating shade locations is looking at your soil. Start by squeezing a handful of soil tightly, then open your fist. If the soil stays lumped together, you likely have a

Dappled shade is the best lighting condition for shade-gardening, allowing for the greatest variety of plantings.

mostly clay soil. If it crumbles apart, you have sandy soil. If it lightly clings together, you just may have the perfect mix of clay, sand, and silt, called "loam."

The last step is determining the acidity or alkalinity of your soil, which you can do by purchasing a soil-test kit or an electronic pH meter, readily available at your local garden center.

Once you understand your shade area's needs, you can begin to take advantage of its strengths and compensate for its weaknesses to build your perfect shade garden.

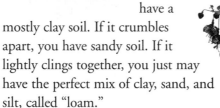

Most flowering shade plants are dependent on some sun to encourage their blooms; this fuchsia thrives on exposure to morning light but welcomes shady protection from the house by the time the sun turns hot in midafternoon.

Afiter assessing your site, the next key question to ask is: what is the purpose of this shade garden? Maybe you love dining alfresco and crave a shaded outdoor dining area under a canopy of trees. Perhaps you once strolled down a beautiful wisteria-draped, trellised walkway at a lovely hotel and you want to create something similar from one area of your yard to another. On a trip to the public gardens, perhaps you were drawn to a mossy garden with a softly bubbling pond because it was so relaxing.

If you don't have an express purpose in mind, there are several ways to develop one. Start by taking a look at your yard as a whole. You might, for example, have plenty of lawn where rambunctious children can play but no spot where adults can sit and talk. Maybe your sun garden is already so bright with colorful flowers that the yard could use a soothing all-green shade foliage garden to provide relief and contrast.

You also might find a purpose in reclaiming the unused spots of your yard where you've left shaded areas largely unplanted. If you plan with an eye to texture and form, you can create visual interest and redefine your yard's boundaries.

Shade gardens are greatly adaptable creations that can take on many personalities. Some of these will come from the way you decide to "decorate" the garden [see Chapter Three, pg. 31]. Decorating, however, will complement function, not create it. Defining a purpose will help you shape a definite plan that you then can adorn.

FUNCTIONAL SHADE GARDENS

(Above) Almost by definition, shade plantings are hardy. What else could bear light traffic while enhancing a garden pathway?

(Left) Bamboo planted in containers provides an elegant backdrop and a moveable privacy screen.

INCREASING LIGHT

Picture a dark corner of the yard occupied by an overgrown 30-foot (9-m) tree and a couple of dense old azaleas drooping to the ground. The fence behind the tree is old, dark wood. The branches overhead are interwoven and so thickly leaved that no light penetrates to the dark ivy carpet below.

Testing the extremes of sun and shade exposure on your planting site with a light meter will help you choose your plantings or adapt the site to plants you already have chosen. Remember that the amount of light doubles as each f-stop increases a full stop.

Such a dark scene might seem unsalvageable, but with good pruning shears, loppers, and a sturdy pole saw, you can make even the dimmest spot attractive and comfortable. Proper pruning is as essential to shade gardening as are water and fertilizer. It benefits not only the plant being pruned but all the plants surrounding it, which can suffer from poor air circulation caused by overgrown trees, shrubs, and ground cover.

There are two main approaches to pruning, and each achieves a different result. One involves topping a plant to control its height and shaving its sides to control its spread. This technique works best with deciduous trees and other plants that readily fill in shaved areas. It is especially effective in giving a distinct, dense shape to a plant. The other method is most helpful in shade situations: it accentuates a plant's natural structure by cutting away or thinning unimportant growth to reveal articulated trunks and limbs. With this second method, you work from the inside out, and sometimes from the bottom up, to "trace" the plant's natural shape. Though a shade garden can benefit from either approach, the most natural look comes from opening up a plant from the inside. It is the preferred method of pruning for most deciduous trees, azaleas, camellias, and other shrubs.

One school of thought holds that you should prune midsummer so you can see your results—and mistakes—quickly. Make sure you check with your local nursery or home garden center expert on recommended pruning times: pruning any species at the wrong time of year is a mistake. A generally safe approach is to do your initial hard pruning—cutting back about a third of the growth—when the tree is going dormant for the winter, then do a lighter touch-up in the summer. Thin out small branches and leaf clumps until you see dappled light hitting the ground below.

Pruning overgrowth is only one of several ways you can bring light to dark areas. Remember that dark fence? It can be painted white or any light pastel color to reflect available light into the garden area. In addition, the dark ivy beneath the old tree can be removed or cut back to allow plantings of bright-colored, shade-tolerant plants such as coleus or impatiens. Surround them with a "mulch" of white pebbles or light-colored bark chips and you will add even more reflection. Finally, don't forget the impact container "visitors" can have. Light-colored pots of azaleas or camellias, or hanging pots of hot-colored impatiens, will survive, thrive, and bring light to any shady space.

If the shade in a certain area is too dense for some of the plantings you desire, prune to let in more light. Also notice how colors pop in dark areas.

PRUNING DECIDUOUS TREES

Most deciduous trees and shrubs—those that annually lose their leaves—benefit from heavy pruning once they have finished blooming or their fruit has fallen. Restrict pruning to once per year; lightly shape as necessary year round. Pruning opens light to the interior of the tree, eliminates deadwood and crossing branches, and creates a classic, upside-down umbrella form. Follow the steps shown for best results:

1 A tree requires pruning when its canopy becomes dense with excess branches, top heavy with new growth, or is diseased.

2 Remove all crossing branches that extend back toward the center of the tree from its outside perimeter.

3 Reduce the number of lateral limbs to increase the amount of light that penetrates the tree. Cut away any dead wood.

4 If the tree itself is too tall, or it bears new growth that is too tall, use a pole pruner to cut back or remove shoots.

5 After pruning, the tree's canopy is uniformly shaped, open to light, and free of all diseased or dead wood.

REDUCING THE EFFECTS OF HOT SUN

A necessary prerequisite to a shady garden is, of course, shade. Those who live in Sunbelt areas or in newly built subdivisions, where the trees are still young and spindly, may think that a shade garden is not feasible. A shade garden may be of more practical use in the hottest climates, but it is possible to achieve nearly anywhere. There are many ways to create shade where none exists, and not all of them require a decade or two for trees to grow.

One simple way to create shade is to buy some large, fast-growing, sun-loving shrubs, such as Scotch broom or lilacs, that quickly branch out. You can plant these in the ground or, for an incredibly quick solution, place them in large containers and arrange them to establish a shady plot. This idea works particularly well if you are planting trees within the same plot; by the time they are established, the potted shrubs can be moved to another location or transplanted into open ground.

Another way to make shade quickly is to buy shade cloth, available at home improvement and garden stores. Shade cloth is woven, screenlike material usually made from plastic but sometimes also metal. Commonly, it comes in mesh sizes offering either 30 percent or 60 percent filtration of the sun's rays. If you already have an arbor or other openwork patio structure, you can affix the shade cloth with small staples to its cross beams.

An arbor, pergola, or other openwork structure can provide the dappled light preferred by most shade plantings in hot, sunny climates.

Another option is to erect a shade cover [see opposite]. The project will take a weekend if you decide to build it from scratch, less time if you decide to purchase a prefabricated kit from a home-improvement center or hardware store and put it together. The trelliswork itself provides some shade, serving as an attractive backdrop and support for such shade-tolerant climbing vines as morning glory, clematis, princess flower, and wisteria.

A lath-covered structure provides shade to you and a ready-made horizontal surface for displaying your potted shade plants.

CONSTRUCTING A SHADE COVER

Shade covers are an attractive focal point for a garden, and they provide a structure on which to display hanging container plants The offset shade cover shown here is made of red cedar, is simple to construct, and can be installed in a weekend. Follow the steps shown to a successful project:

1 Cut all lumber to length. At the top of each post, attach two support rails and their braccs with bolts and lag screws.

Required Materials:

2	10-ft. (3-m)	4×4 (89×89 mm)	Posts
4	2-ft. (60-cm)	2×6 (38×140 mm)	Support rails
2	8-in. (20-cm)	2×4 (38×89 mm)	Braces
2	16-in. (40-cm)	2×4 (38×89 mm)	Braces
2	8-ft. (243-cm)	2×6 (38×140 mm)	Ledgers
23	3-ft. (90-cm)	2×2 (38×38 mm)	Shade stiles
4	Bags	Fence-post concrete mix	
4	3/8×7 1/2-in. (10×190-mm) Bolts, nuts, washers		
80	1/8×3-in. (3×75-mm) Lag screws		
1	1/2-gal. (2-l) Each: Primer/sealer and paint		

2 To the face of each support rail, predrill and attach a ledger with lag screws.

3 Space the stiles two stile widths apart. Predrill holes and attach them with lag screws at the top.

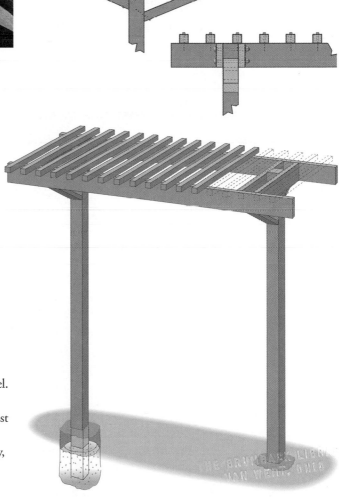

4 Erect the assembly into predug footing holes, 18 in. (45 cm) deep, brace, and level. Pour two bags of fence-post concrete mix around each post and water. Backfill the holes and, when the concrete is dry, prime and paint the finished shade cover.

Decorating with Shade Plants

Decorating might seem like an odd term to use for gardening, but landscape designers invoke it frequently when discussing choices of plants for a particular situation. They refer to specialized garden areas, such as the typical shade garden, as "rooms," an imagery that works quite well when you think about it. Tall canopy trees act as a ceiling; lawn, ground cover, or hardscaping as carpet or floor. Small trees, shrubs, and plants that surround the area are the room's decor. Choosing plants and a design scheme for your garden, then, is much the same as decorating any room of your house. Just as you enjoy being surrounded by furnishings and artwork that make you feel comfortable, your shade garden plants should be selected to give you the same pleasure.

Like a house, a shade garden can be designed in many styles. You may want to choose a distinct theme, such as a wild woodland bower, a formal Italianate garden, or a serene Oriental garden. You also should choose a color palette—bright flowers and foliage, pale flowers and green foliage, a range of green foliage only, or all-white flowers, for instance. Think about the plants that will add to the atmosphere you want to evoke. You also may want to address problems, such as lighting up a dark corner with brighter colors or creating an enticing pathway from one part of the yard to another. All these considerations comprise the art of decorating with plants.

In the pages that follow, you'll find ideas and advice on how to approach creating a shade landscape, including how to select a theme and a color scheme that suits your goal. There are useful tips about decorating with trees, shrubs, and ground cover, using overhead space creatively through vertical planting, and augmenting your shade garden with container planting.

Don't forget to take a stroll through the Encyclopedia of Shade Plants [see pg. 79]. It will let you know if that beguiling fuchsia or the coy fern crooking its fronds at you will grow in your shade garden's light and soil conditions.

This serene waterfall garden simply would not be possible without the inclusion of moisture-loving shade plants.

CREATING A SHADE LANDSCAPE

Once you have decided where you want your shade garden and you have a general idea of its purpose, you're ready to design its look.

Successful gardens are seldom random. The interplay of elements all must be calculated carefully, regardless of how "wild" or natural looking the intended result. Generally, a garden looks best with variations of height, leaf styles, textures, and colors.

When professional designers look at a landscape, they think about focal points—where the eye should be drawn first—then which plants are striking or unusual. Once the focal points are determined, the challenge is to enhance the chosen plants with secondary plantings that also complements each other.

One of the best ways to factor these concerns into your design is to create a simple "bubble" diagram—taking a piece of paper and drawing bubbles (or circles) to broadly indicate where plants should be situated in the bed or border. First, "bubble in" all existing plants and structures, then take your plan to the garden area and start "placing" your desired plants, allowing space on the diagram for their mature size and spread. With the completed bubble plan in hand, you can visualize how the grouping will look and get a good sense of how many plants will be needed.

Better still is a good computer software program dedicated to landscape or garden design. These programs allow you to rough sketch your site, place all sorts of structures on it, design fencing and hardscaping, and, of course, lay out your shade garden. As you determine the exact plant you want to put in a spot, simply open that plant's file, select a color and maturity of the plant, and pop it into your bed.

Whether you decide to use a computer or tried-and-true manual methods, mapping out your landscape plan is the best way to ensure you'll have a beautiful and well-designed shade garden.

When planting ferns or any permanent plants, keep in mind that they tend to spread more in shade.

A garden looks its best when plantings vary in height, leaf style, texture, and color. Despite a natural appearance, there always is an underlying organization behind every successful garden.

DESIGNING A
SHADE GARDEN

Technology speeds up the already-simple process of designing a shade garden. Modern computer landscaping programs, available through many software retailers, contain easy-to-use tools and predrawn plant symbols to help you visualize the finished results. Follow the specific software program's instructions for best results. Traditional methods use the same steps as most computer programs, beginning with a large, conceptual design, then adapting it to the site. Careful measurements are the key to good results regardless of the method employed. Begin your design by following these steps:

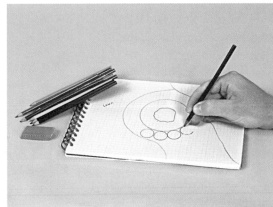

1 Roughly sketch the garden site, using circles, or "bubbles," to allocate space for groups of plantings. Try a number of versions until the bed begins to work. Colored pencils help visualize the foliage and flowers in the bed.

2 Measure the site and carefully note its dimensions. Using graph paper, transfer the site to paper and scale all of the elements in each bubble.

3 To use a landscape software program on a home computer, enter your bubble diagram and site measurements as directed by the program. When placing plants in the scale drawing of the site, choose from the software's library of flowers, shrubs, and trees. Try different combinations, varying the height and maturity of the plantings. When the design is complete, print it out along with a shopping list (if the program includes such a feature).

CREATING A COLOR SCHEME

The myriad possibilities for a shade garden can overwhelm anyone. Deciding on a theme or a color scheme first can help focus your plans and make shopping for plants much easier. It's also a step toward "designing" rather than just planting.

When landscape designers take on projects, they consider several factors. Complementing architecture is a primary consideration if the shade garden will be near existing structures. The style of the architecture—such as Spanish Colonial, Federalist, or Georgian—will inform your planting choices. For example, an English cottage almost demands an abundantly flowering border and masses of roses. A Mediterranean-style hacienda looks best with flowering vines and silver tones. Designing a garden to complement architecture can create visual harmony and enhance the look of both the house and the garden.

You can create themes based on color as well. A foliage garden devoted to subtly shifting shades of green and green-gold will lend a sophisticated air, as will green foliage punctuated by all-white flowers. If color is your preference, think about whether you prefer soft pastels or brilliant, eye-popping colors—generally, it's best not to combine the two. A color wheel also can help you create a design palette. Colors opposite each other on the wheel, such as blues and red-oranges, are contrasting colors, which create visual tension and drama. Those close to one another on the wheel (like blue-reds, pinks, and purples) are harmonizing colors that add visual unity and softness.

As you plan, take into account the quality of the shade garden's light. In deep shade, dark colors go dead, while whites and yellows pop. Bright colors virtually dance in dappled and light shade. Warm colors such as orange-red, orange, and yellow bring intimacy to a deep-shade area, while cool violets, blues, and blue-reds appear to recede, thereby adding depth to a shallow space.

Playing with color is one of the most fascinating gardening pastimes. Selecting a theme, either elaborate or simple, also streamlines and focuses your designing and purchasing tasks.

Successfully combining colors frequently involves using two colors from the same quadrant of the color wheel (such as purple and red) or opposing colors (such as yellow and purple)—or combines the two approaches.

USING A COLOR WHEEL

C olor wheels, readily available at hobby and art stores, are used by artists and designers to visualize the colors they will use for paintings and other projects. Flower gardeners also can benefit by planning with color in mind. The wheel presents the primary colors—red, yellow, and blue—interspersed with their complements—orange, green, and violet. It also is divided into so-called cool and warm palettes. Follow these easy steps to use a color wheel when you choose plants for your shade garden landscape:

1 Consult the color wheel as you choose flower colors. Make your first selection among the primary colors, as a focus for the planting. Strong, vibrant colors draw the eye, while pastels tend to blend into the background.

2 Next, make a foliage plant selection from a complementary color (directly across the wheel from the primary chosen). By selecting a complement to the primary, you assure a good color match and allow the feature plant to reveal its color by comparison. Here, a variegated green and yellow broadleaf was chosen.

3 Fill out the planting by adding colors adjacent to the primary that was selected. For this group, pink flowers and yellow and green foliage completes the selection.

VERTICAL PLANTINGS

As you develop your planting scheme, don't limit yourself to ground- or shrub-level plants. Vertical gardening is particularly conducive to shade since the source of the shade often provides a built-in support for vertical plantings such as vines and container gardens. If trees provide your overstory, suspend hanging baskets of abundant flowers from branches to add color and depth at eye level. If your shade is created by an arbor or overhead trellis, soften the edges of the structure by training sun-loving vines such as bougainvillea up posts and across the top. If your arbor is very open and does not provide much shade, a substantial vining plant, such as wisteria, can create shade.

There also are shade-tolerant vines that can enhance both living and man-made elements of your shade garden. Most ivies will scale the trunk of a tree happily, but you must be careful to contain the ivy's growth so it does not engulf the tree entirely.

The source of shade, which often includes vertical structures, also provides a support for climbing plants to be displayed, which in turn create even more shade.

Hanging containers [see opposite] are versatile additions to a shade garden. They can provide focal points, create intimacy, bring in spots of color, and accentuate the twist of a beautiful tree branch or the beauty of an outdoor structure. Change the look and mood of your container garden by changing the annuals in them to announce the season.

With the right humidity, either natural or supplied through a misting system, you also can "attach" some unusual plantings to a tree. The staghorn fern and the orchid are epiphytes, meaning they are perfectly suited to open shade that maintains some humidity. Attach them to a tree trunk with soft cotton cord; the plant will send roots into the tree bark and the cotton cord will biodegrade over time.

Many shade plants, though happy in their shady conditions, will ramble upward to seek the sun. Control this tendency towards legginess and spread with an occasional pruning.

INSTALLING HANGING PLANTERS ON TREES

Hanging planters from trees is a natural addition to any shade garden. Use the correct technique to suspend them to prevent damaging the tree. Remember that hanging containers are free to move in the wind and that this movement can cause the hanging hardware to chafe and saw through the limb, killing it and exposing the tree to disease. Avoid this potential problem by installing a loose collar around the cord or chain, following these simple steps:

1 Thread hanger cord through vinyl tubing large enough so the cord freely moves inside it. The tubing should be at least as long as the tree limb's circumference.

2 Securely attach one end of the hanger cord to the planter's hanging chain. An "S" or other swivel attachment is best since it will allow the container to move freely in the wind.

3 Rest the tubing on the top of the limb, balancing it evenly. Draw down the loose end of the hanger cord and affix it to the planter.

4 The completed hanging planter installation allows the basket to move freely within the tubing sheath without damaging the tree limb's sensitive bark.

GROUND COVER FOR SHADE LOCATIONS

Mounding ground covers provide a spot of softness between the stones of a pathway.

Ground covers are the most versatile and indispensable of shade-garden plants. They are the great unifiers in borders and beds, creating a sea of color out of which spring perennials and shrubs. They also can be used alone as a fine transition from sunny lawn to shady sites or to cover densely shaded areas where even shade plants do not fare well. They are easy to plant and very easy to maintain since their ground-shading quality retains moisture. Once established, they need little fertilizing. If you have a lot of shaded ground, ground covers can be an economical and attractive way to landscape. They will need some pruning and trimming to keep them under control, and for the most part, you will want to choose non-invasive varieties, unless your area is vast.

You plant ground cover the same way you plant annuals or perennials. Most ground covers prefer a light, rich soil that retains moisture, although some, such as creeping Jenny and certain ivies, do well in dry situations. In addition to selecting for soil compatibility, check that the water and soil requirements of the ground cover match those of any shrubs, annuals, or perennials you plan to plant in the area.

When you have selected your ground cover, prepare the soil by incorporating compost, leaf mold, or peat moss and a scattering of all-purpose, slow-release fertilizer, tilling the entire area to a depth of 8–10 inches (20–25 cm). Rake the bed smooth; level and water thoroughly a day or so before planting to allow the soil to settle. Because ground covers send out shoots that root where they touch soil, it's essential that the bed be well prepared. Your particular ground cover choice will have specific spacing requirements [see Encyclopedia of Shade Plants, pg. 79]. Use them to determine the number of plants required.

Dig properly spaced planting holes in a checkerboard pattern. Avoid creating distinct rows. Until the plants grow together, cover the exposed soil surface between them with an inch (3 cm) or two (6 cm) of mulch to squelch weeds and keep the moisture level high. Pull out any weeds that do sprout as soon as you spot them.

Many ground covers are naturally invasive; take advantage of this growth habit to create great effects.

CREATING A SHADY STONE WALKWAY

Natural stone walkways are an appealing addition to any shade setting. They invite visitors to stroll through the shade garden, and they provide easy access for maintenance. Simple stone-on-sand paths are easily installed in a weekend and require few tools and skills. Soften the new path by planting a spreading ground cover between the stones and allow it to fill in the spaces. Follow these steps to create an attractive path:

2 After all the stones have been laid, sweep sand into the spaces between them using a push broom. Soak the area with misted water to settle the stones, then plant ground cover in the joints between the stones.

1 Mark the path and excavate it to a depth of 8 in. (20 cm). Fill it with 4–6 in. (10–15 cm) of loose sand. Level and rake until smooth. Bed the stones into the sand, then tap down gently.

3 At the margins of the path, prepare the soil for planting by adding amendments and organic compost. Loosen and rake the bed.

4 Set taller plants to the rear, away from the path, and shorter species near the edge. Depending on the effect desired, plants may overgrow the path or create a distinct edge alongside the border.

SHRUBS, TREES, AND STANDARDS

Trees, shrubs, and standards—shrubs and vines pruned and trained to function as treelike plantings—form a shade garden's striking framework or foundation, against which perennials, annuals, and bulbs put on their shows. Trees and shrubs don't need to be the spear carriers relegated to the background of the performance, however. There are trees, shrubs, and standards that flower, fruit, and produce seasonal color with the best of the perennials, so indulge yourself when designing them into your shade garden.

Most home gardeners inherit previous homeowners' tree choices and must deal with them as best they can. If you are planting a bare lot, you have the delight of choosing deep-rooted shade trees that generously share their space with other plantings. Some of the best and most beautiful include a well-pruned weeping silver pear, some maples, honey locust, Russian olive, Carolina silverbell, Juneberry, golden raintree, and American smoketree.

Well-chosen, tall-growing trees form the overstory of your garden, while smaller trees can provide seasonal color and a striking contrast. Some of the best for shade include sourwood, with its sprays of white bells and bright fall color; finely textured and brilliantly toned Japanese maples; Japanese cherries and plums; crab apples; laburnum; and small magnolias. If your shade is dappled or gets sun part of the day, consider a dwarf fruit tree such as a crab apple, but set it out in a pot so that you can easily transport it to sunnier climes if the experiment doesn't go as planned.

Shrubs are one of the largest group of shade plants, adding to the mid-height and lower levels a certain heft and sense of permanence to what otherwise would be the relative delicacy of perennials and annuals. These include the ever-popular camellia and azalea, as well as hydrangea, red buckeye, hollies, Japanese spicebush, rose-of-Sharon, and disanthus. Some of these, in fact, grow large enough to provide shade all on their own. An understory composed of several small trees and some striking shrubs can provide year-round color if you choose varieties that either flower or have foliage that changes color at different points in the year.

Shrubs and trees come in many shapes and sizes. Good design comes from juxtaposing a variety of shapes or repeating similar shapes as space allows.

ontainer gardens always seem like a natural for a patio or other hardscaped area, but beautiful terra-cotta, stone, enamel, and wood pots also can serve you in many ways in your shade garden. For one thing, their mobility is a great advantage, and their ability to hold versatile plantings can give your shade garden new and unexpected looks.

The mobility of container gardens means that you can move in temporary color, either with shade-loving annuals or even sun-loving flowers. Most sun lovers, such as daisies, coreopsis, petunias, and marigolds, can tolerate shade, even deep shade, for short periods of time. Once they begin to droop, simply take the pot back into the sun where the flowers will quickly rejuvenate. Container plantings such as azaleas also can be brought in to enhance a shade area with their foliage when their blooms are spent.

Where your shade is filtered by deciduous trees, or where you have partial or full sun part of the day, observe the changes in the light patterns over time [see Evaluating a Shade Location, pg. 24]. Areas that are very shady during the rest of the year may be sunny for two months in midsummer. In spring, until your deciduous trees bud, your shady garden may receive a great deal of cool sun. Your container gardens can reflect each season, which is particularly useful if you have planted your permanent garden only for a specific season's show.

Container plantings also serve another very useful function—they give structure and focus to a garden bed. Setting containers of various heights and styles throughout your shade beds, hanging them from tree limbs, using a large one as a focal point, or placing one in a spot you'd like to emphasize are options that can be achieved more effectively than with permanent plantings.

As avid container gardeners will tell you, one of the best reasons to invest in beautiful pots and engage in container planting is the constant array of opportunities they pose. You'll be looking at your garden with new eyes every season.

CONTAINER PLANTINGS FOR SHADE

These terra-cotta planters lend an air of formality to a shade garden. The plantings are well chosen for the sizes of their containers and for their cool, pink tones, which come alive against the lush dark-green landscape.

W

ith plans in hand, you're ready to get your hands dirty. This chapter is devoted to the process of actually setting in the various shade plants that will make up your new garden.

First up are the basics of installing a simple watering system to keep your water-loving shade plants happily moist. Next we discuss how to install vertical supports for hanging plants and vines and posts for container plantings—the hardscaping of the shade garden bed. For special interest, you'll learn how to install a "wet zone" that adds atmosphere to many shady themes, including the Oriental garden, the woodland or rustic garden, and the formal garden.

Once the infrastructure is in place, you can begin to plant. We take you through the process—how to set out your plants with proper spacing, how to work with the design, and, finally, how to arrange the plantings—from smallest to tallest.

> The keys to a successful shade garden lie in the right soil, supports, and proper watering systems

Planting in Shade

We begin with planting annuals in the shade for quick color and as filler while your slow-growing plants mature. Perennials, the staples of the shade garden, come next, with emphasis on proper soil and spacing for their size at maturity. That rounds out the colorful flowers.

Finally come shrubs, trees, and ferns. Shrubs provide additional structure to a shade bed and can provide wonderful seasonal shows of color. Trees provide an overstory to smaller, understory trees that thrive in the shade cast by the canopy above. Last but not least we discuss ferns, the quintessential shade garden planting. For each plant group, we provide complete step-by-step instructions on how to install these plantings in the shade garden you've planned.

Before planting, set out your chosen plants in their planting location for about a week— leaving them in their nursery containers. If they thrive in their new home, you're ready to set them into the ground.

VERTICAL SUPPORTS

The best time to lay your shade garden's foundation—which includes arbors, trellises, posts for hanging plants, decorative stones and boulders, irrigation systems, or all of the above—is before you begin planting.

Water delivery has become something of an art form in home gardens. There are a variety of exotic misters, spitters, and mini-sprinklers that humidify the air, water hanging plants, and otherwise keep the atmosphere and soil suitably moist [see In-ground Irrigation Systems, pg. 46, and Drip-Irrigation Systems, pg. 48].

Equally as vast are the choices for vertical supports and structures, which come in almost every shape, material, and size imaginable. Many climbing shade plants are perfect choices for arbors [see Constructing a Shade Cover, pg. 29]. The roots of clematis, for example, need cool, moist shade, while the sun-loving vine quickly shoots up the posts to open its flowers in the light.

Other climbers with heavy foliage may need more stability in the form of a trellis. Trellises have an open-air design, often with crisscrossing diagonal slats made from thin strips of treated wood or vinyl. If used for a container planting, the trellis should be installed before the soil and plants are added. Affix the trellis to the inside of the container using brass screws for wood containers and gardening tape for terra-cotta pots. Make sure to place the container with trellis a few inches (approximately 8 cm) away from any structure to ensure good air circulation, especially because most shade plants grow in conditions more conducive to mildew and other diseases than do sun lovers.

A container trellis is a perfect choice for such shade-loving plants as bougainvillea, climbing hydrangea, morning glory, and many species of ivy.

Other natural "supporters" of shade plants are hanging planters [see Installing Hanging Planters on Trees, pg. 37] and plant posts that display both hanging and tabletop pots [see opposite].

A plant post is a charming decorative and functional element in a shade garden. Shelving holds decorative pots filled with a series of small shade-loving plants; dowels support wire baskets filled with dried moss, lightweight potting soil, and lush trailing plants that add dimension to the structure. Because the plant post is meant to be a permanent fixture, carefully consider its site and the plantings you intend to use before pouring concrete for it.

A plant post allows you to change your shade garden every day. Depending on the post's location, it may allow you to bring in some sun lovers for a few hours.

BUILDING A PLANT POST

Required Materials:

1	6-ft. (180-cm)	4×4 (89 × 89 mm)	Post
4	12-in. (30-cm)	1×8 (19 × 184 mm)	Shelves
2	18-in. (45-cm)	¾-in. (19-mm)	Dowel
1	Sack	Fence-post concrete mix	
1	Bottle	Woodworker's glue	
4	L-bracket shelf supports and fasteners		
1	1 qt. (1 l)	Paint	

A plant post provides an attractive focal point in shady nooks or other background areas of a landscape. It raises potted plants and hanging baskets above ground level, "framing" them against a backdrop of shrubs and the underfoliage of trees. Constructing and installing a plant post is a quick and simple project, requiring only a drill, a saw, and your time. Allow a couple of hours for construction and another for installing the post. Follow these easy instructions:

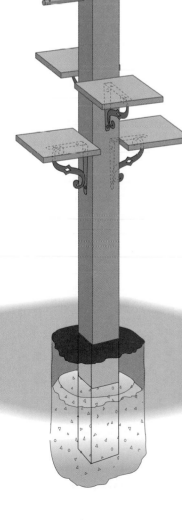

1 Drill two ¾-in. (19-mm) holes in the post, spaced 6 and 24 in. (15 and 60 cm) from the top of the post, on opposite faces.

2 Thread the dowels through the post, and when they are centered, glue them into place.

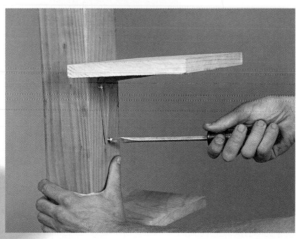

3 Install shelves to shelf brackets, then to the post. Position each shelf 18 in. (45 cm) below the dowel above it. Prime the entire assembly prior to installation with exterior sealer or paint.

4 Dig a footing 18 in. (45 cm) deep, then level and brace the post and fill with concrete.

IN-GROUND IRRIGATION SYSTEMS

Anyone who has spent time watering with a hose, sprinklers, or a watering can will appreciate the ease of care provided by an in-ground irrigation system on an automatic timer. Such systems are more than a convenience—they provide an assured supply of precious water to your shade plantings.

Other than the work of trenching, the skills needed to install an in-ground system are surprisingly simple. Nearly anyone can cut PVC pipe using hand-held pipe cutting shears. Assembly is equally simple: just prime and apply glue to both sides of each joint, then twist the two together and allow them to dry.

Always install a backflow preventer at the connection to the water supply to prevent any potential risk of water from your irrigation system siphoning into your household water.

Planning for the system is the most important step. First, determine the water pressure available at the water-supply connection. This is done in either of two ways: measure the pressure directly by attaching an inexpensive water pressure meter to an existing hose bib or faucet, or measure the quantity of water produced in a bucket from an unrestricted flow in one minute. Then, with this information, calculate the total number of "circuits"—separately timed water-supply lines—that are needed for the number of plantings you plan. It's a good idea to provide separate circuits for bedding plants, for shrubs, and for trees, due to their differing watering needs.

Sprinkler heads and other irrigation fixtures are available in many flow rates and dispersal patterns. Choose ones suited to your plants. For example, a large shrub may require five gallons (19 l) of water each irrigation, while a small annual plant may need only a quart (.9 l). Both can receive the correct amount of water in a five-minute period if you select a 1-gallon-per-minute (3.8-l-per-minute) bubbler for the shrub and a ⅛-gallon-per-minute (.5-l-per-minute) drip emitter for the annual.

In-ground irrigation systems are best installed prior to planting your shade garden. They may be expanded or adjusted easily as your needs change.

1 From your water-supply line and backflow-prevention valve, trench and run 1-in. (25-mm) Schedule 40 pipe to the control-valve location. Install a ¾-in. (18-mm) reducing bushing at the valve. Mount control valves below grade in regions where freezing temperatures are likely.

2 Install a separate control valve for each water circuit. Use a ½-in. (12-mm) reducing bushing between each valve and the lines that run to the sprinkler heads or drip emitters.

INSTALLING AN IN-GROUND IRRIGATION SYSTEM

Permanent watering systems make caring for a shade garden easier and can ensure that all of your plants receive adequate moisture according to a programmed schedule. Installing such systems, while physically demanding, is easy to do and requires basic tools. Plan your system carefully, using the literature and worksheets readily available at your garden retail or hardware store. Allow for future expansion. Follow these simple steps to automate irrigation in your shade garden:

3 Cut pipe to length, using a PVC pipe-cutting tool, then join sections using two-step primer and adhesive. Allow joints to dry.

4 Where each irrigation head is planned, install a 90° "street tee" or "ell" fitting with slip joints to the pipe and a threaded coupler to the riser.

5 Install sprinkler spray housings or drip-system hose couplers atop each riser, using three wraps of teflon tape around each threaded fitting.

6 Turn on the gate valve and sprinkler manifold to clear the line of debris, then turn off and install spray heads or drip lines. Finally, set the controller.

DRIP-IRRIGATION SYSTEMS

In recent years, drip irrigation has become very popular as a means of watering landscape gardens. The technology has improved rapidly, and many of the early problems have been overcome. Shade gardeners should consider drip irrigation if their plantings are extensive or have special needs.

A bubbler delivers water gently and at a slow rate, keeping moisture off the tops of foliage.

Drip irrigation, put simply, permits plants to be watered in a rifle-shot rather than shotgun manner. Small fixtures, called emitters, are placed at the base of each plant and attached to the water supply by thin, flexible tubing. This tubing, in turn, is attached to larger-diameter tubing or a drip-line coupler.

Among the many benefits of drip irrigation is the potential for water conservation; all of the water reaches the plant and none is lost to runoff. The amount of water released is controlled by the gardener's choice of emitters, each of which is flow rated to release a precise amount of water in a fixed period of time. The use of an automatic time valve that can be set to run at a specific time and for a set duration, controls the amount of water delivered to each plant.

While this description may sound complicated, in practice it is very simple. Drip systems may be attached to existing in-ground irrigation systems or to a hose bib already located in the garden [see opposite].

Drip systems are well suited to shade gardens, with their variety of plants each requiring individual attention. Moisture lovers can be watered heavily and frequently, while dry-shade plants can receive irrigation less frequently. Moisture sensors can be included in the system to turn off the irrigation when it rains or to trigger a watering when the soil becomes too dry.

Whether you water with a drip-irrigation system, an in-ground system, or by hand, remember that your watering should be guided by your plants' needs, your soil conditions, and the prevailing weather and humidity. In short, this means that even a fully automatic system requires you to monitor it: drip lines can become clogged, wet weather can saturate the soil and require the system to be turned off temporarily, or a dry spell can make more frequent and abundant watering necessary.

Rely on the expert help at your garden store or home-improvement center to guide you in selecting a system or systems right for your needs. These retailers have staff knowledgeable about the various systems on the market and they frequently can give you helpful tips and advice on combining them and installing them.

A drip-irrigation-system sprayer head delivers a light watering in a circular fashion.

A SIMPLE DRIP SYSTEM

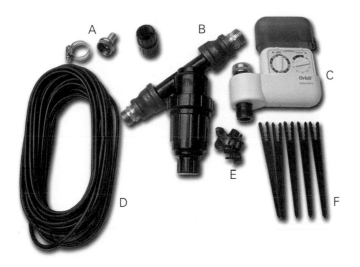

A
B
C
E
D
F

Create drip systems quickly and inexpensively by attaching battery-controlled timers and filters to nearby faucets or hose bibs. Drip irrigation conserves water by emitting just the needed amount to each plant. A single system can water up to 30 plants, depending on the water pressure. Follow these steps:

Required Components:

A   Couplers and fittings
B   Drip-irrigation water filter
C   Battery-timed hose-bib
    irrigation valve
D   Drip-irrigation line hose
E   Drip emitters
F   Line-placement stakes

1 Couple timer valve to hose bib, then install an in-line water filter to prevent clogged lines. Bushings may be needed where threads do not match exactly.

2 From the filter, attach the drip-supply hose. This large-diameter hose carries pressurized water to the attachment points on each of the individual drip lines. It may have several joints and junctions, depending on your garden.

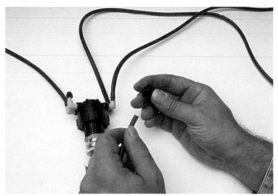

3 Wherever a drip line is needed, terminate the supply hose with a drip-line coupler, available in 2-, 4-, and 8-connection models. Attach 1/4-in. (6-mm) supply tubing and one or more emitters.

SHADE WATER GARDENS

Shade gardens are perfect environments for water features, whether a pond, fountain, cascade, or aquatic garden. If you think of a woodland setting or even a traditional Japanese garden, you can imagine a cool damp area covered with mosses and other moisture-loving shade plantings. A "wet zone," a variation on the classic aquatic garden [see opposite], is just as easily achieved with a few supplies from your local garden store or home-improvement center.

Though it looks natural, this aquatic garden is man-made with plants that either require constant moisture or can survive when rooted underwater. They are planted in special aquatic soils, held in submerged, weighted containers.

Like an aquatic garden, a wet zone requires a preformed plastic pool liner, usually irregularly shaped. These liners often are installed as water ponds planted with water lilies and stocked with small fish. For a wet zone, the liner is filled with very sandy soil kept damp to foster water-loving plants. A pumping system buried at the bottom of the pool recycles water that is misted several times a day over the sand to keep the surface moist and the water aerated and fresh.

Plants that thrive in a wet zone include such water lovers as rushes, astilbes, and Siberian iris. Moist-soil ferns such as ostrich plume fern, royal fern, and marsh fern contribute height. Lower areas can be filled in with moss collected from other parts of your yard or woodland areas. Once the plantings have been set in, enough water should be added so that it flows down and pools into the rock layer. This will allow it to be taken up through the intake pipe and lightly misted over the plants to keep the zone and nearby environment continually and consistently moist.

Whether an aquatic garden or a wet zone, your new water garden will give you a cool and unusual shady retreat on hot summer days.

Any type of water garden can be equipped with a pump and intake pipe for misting the plants, ensuring them a continually and consistently moist environment.

BUILDING AN AQUATIC GARDEN

Water gardens look spectacular, add a special element to any landscape, and can be created easily using readily available materials and plants. In difficulty, it requires a bit more skill than potting petunias, but it boasts major paybacks in satisfaction. Follow these steps for a successful project:

2 Insert the premolded liner into the hole. Use a straightedge and level to check the installation.

1 Dig and level a hole of the desired shape and depth; premolded plastic pond liners are available in a variety of shapes. Be sure to set the pond or tub on a level and compacted base of builder's sand.

3 Fill the liner with water to bed it securely into the sand. Frame the top edge of the basin with river rock or other stone. Dry stack the stones in a double-height row to create the desired appearance.

4 Fill the pond with tap water and insert a special aquatic filter (similar to a fish-tank filter) to aerate and keep the water fresh; hide or bury the filter's supply-line hose beneath the stones.

5 Plant aquatic plants in a mix of potting soil and sand, topped with a 1-in. (25-mm) layer of coarse pea gravel. Weight the pots and settle them gently into the pond.

PREPARING TO PLANT

If you have sketched out a detailed plan in advance [see Creating a Shade Landscape, pg. 32] and researched your plant choices, you are ready to plant—almost. The most important aspect of preparation is making sure you have properly amended your soil for the needs of the plants you have chosen.

Testing your soil for clay, silt, and sand content and for pH level is easy [see opposite]. If your soil is not loose enough, add leaf mold or organic compost to lighten it. Peat moss will help lighten it and also acidify the soil. Limestone and crushed oyster shells will help neutralize excess acidity. Slow-release nitrogen fertilizers will help your new plantings compete with established trees and shrubs.

Next, place the plants you've chosen, still in their containers, in the spots indicated on your plan and leave them there for three to five days to make sure they are well suited to their sites. If some of them start to flag, simply move them to a different location—they will rebound without lasting harm. Once you're ready to plant, place the large and permanent before the small and transitory—which means that trees, tall shrubs, and shrub standards go in first (and in that order), followed by smaller shrubs and ferns, and then perennials. Finally, use annuals to fill in spaces that young perennials eventually will take over. Start at the back of the bed and work forward, which will allow you to loosen the soil you've just trampled.

Let's say that you're laying out a lush camellia, azalea, and fern garden. If there is a plant you want to spotlight or make the focal point of the bed, plant it first. It's usually the plant that will grow tallest—in this case, the camellia. Place it anywhere between the middle and the back of the bed. Then measure forward from the center of the trunk of the camellia to where the center of the next-largest plants—the ferns—will be placed, allowing them sufficient room for their ultimate spreads.

If your fern choices grow to midsize, you can plant some of them behind the camellia to provide a finely textured backdrop and contrast to the camellia's smooth, glossy leaves and elegant spring flowers. In front of the camellia, plant azaleas in colors that are complementary to it. Fill in the spaces at the very front of the border with annuals.

Many shade-loving plants, like most plants, prefer a loose, humus-rich soil that holds some moisture but drains well. Because shade-garden soil tends to retain moisture, make sure it is well amended to promote drainage.

PERFORMING A SOIL TEST

Soil tests measure four properties of importance to shade-garden plants: the relative levels of nitrogen (N), phosphorus (P), and potassium (K); and the acid-alkaline balance of the soil—it's so-called pH—on a scale in which 7.0 is neutral, lower numbers indicate acidity, and higher numbers alkalinity. Follow the steps shown to obtain a good sample for testing with a simple reactive test kit, available in most garden stores:

1 Use a shovel or spade to dig a hole at least 16 in. (40 cm) deep and 12 in. (30 cm) in diameter. Avoid testing surface soil from your garden—since plant roots draw nutrients from subsurface soil, the reading may be inaccurate.

2 Using a clean trowel and collecting cup, take a soil sample from the side of the hole, about 12 in. (30 cm) down. Follow the test-kit's instructions to measure the nutrients and pH of the sample.

3 If the area to be tested is large, collect separate soil samples from several locations in clean, glass collecting jars, then mix them together thoroughly before performing the test.

PLANTING ANNUAL COLOR IN SHADE

As shrubs and perennials are your shade garden's foundation, annuals are its accessories. An annual, technically, is a plant that completes its life cycle, from germination to flowering to seeding to expiration, within a year. Most annuals are sun lovers, but some are well adapted to the shade, particularly if the climate is warm.

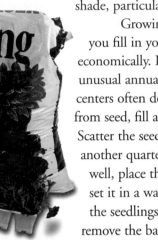

Growing annuals from seed lets you fill in your garden early and economically. It also opens up a world of unusual annuals that nurseries and garden centers often don't stock. To start annuals from seed, fill a flat with potting soil. Scatter the seeds on top, cover them with another quarter-inch (6 mm) of soil, water well, place the flat in a plastic bag, and set it in a warm, dark area. In no time the seedlings will emerge. Immediately remove the bag, set the flat out where it will get the sun's warmth and light, and water daily. When spring comes, you will be able to plant your annuals outdoors after you harden them—a process by which plants are gradually acclimated to an outdoor setting by being left outside for longer and longer periods each day.

If time doesn't allow starting plants from seed, you can buy annuals in six-packs or single containers for planting in pots [see opposite] or open ground. Most annuals prefer fairly loose, rich loam that holds moisture. Plant shade-loving annuals slightly farther apart than indicated for the species—maybe a quarter to half again the spacing requirement—since they generally spread to maximize their exposure to sunlight and will quickly fill in the bed.

Annuals tend to flower freely, since that is the source of their seeds and therefore their regeneration. In the shade garden, they provide bursts of color and happily fill in spaces between young perennials that have not yet reached full size.

PLANTING ANNUALS IN MOVEABLE CONTAINERS

The great thing about annuals is that they look terrific as blooming nursery starts and only get better as they fill out and continue their flowering throughout the season. Planting them is easy, especially given how dramatic an impact they quickly make on a garden. Follow these simple steps:

2 Gently compact the soil, adding as needed to reach 1–2 in. (25–50 mm) below the rim of the container.

3 Carefully ease your starts out of their nursery containers and gently loosen the soil around the roots with a hand fork, breaking up any roots that encircle the rootball.

1 Select and fill your planter with a medium-texture bedding soil or potting mix.

4 With a trowel, dig planting holes large enough for the roots of the starts. Leave a space between plants to allow for root and plant growth.

5 Compact the potting mix around each rootball; add more soil as necessary to cover the roots completely and stabilize the plants. Water immediately after planting.

PLANTING PERENNIALS IN SHADE

Perennials are plants that, once established in the ground, continue to grow season after season. Although so-called tender perennials are not very hardy in extreme cold, the value of most perennials lies in their permanence.

Shade-loving perennials come in all shapes, sizes, and flowering habits. Some, such as the hostas, are prized for their foliage. Perennials, however, are among the best sources of flowering color in a shade garden, though most tend to blossom only once a year, often in spring. They are available to suit just about any soil condition—dry, moist, or wet—and any shade intensity.

For best flowering, plant shade-loving perennials in areas that receive at least partial or half shade. Too little exposure to sunlight will encourage the growth of foliage rather than colorful blooms.

The two major concerns of planting shade perennials are soil and spacing. Shade perennials require holes that are much wider and deeper than those for annuals—something on the order of a shrub-sized hole or one that is about the diameter of the plant's spread at maturity. Give each plant a solid supply of phosphorus and potash by mixing the amendments with soil at the bottom of the holes and incorporating them into the surrounding soil the roots ultimately will penetrate. These essential elements cling to soil particles and do not move well, so make sure you have put them right where the roots can use them.

Proper spacing is important for several reasons. First, shade plants tend to spread more than plants in the sun, in an effort to collect as much available light as they can for photosynthesis. Also, shade environments, particularly moist and wet ones, tend to lack good air circulation. Poor circulation is a breeding ground for disease among shade plants, particularly fungal infections. Finally, perennials can experience substantial growth over time, so they need adequate elbow room. Space them according to their size at maturity so they just graze the leaves of their nearby companions. If sparseness concerns you, use annuals to fill in until the perennials mature. If you prefer, you can get away with closer plantings of young perennials by planting some in the ground in pots large enough to accommodate some root growth. As the bed fills in, dig up the potted perennials and plant them elsewhere.

Set perennials into the ground as you would any other planting [see opposite], backfilling with garden soil that has been amended to suit the plants you have chosen.

When adding fertilizer to perennial shade plants, make sure to dig it in where the roots can use it. To determine the spread of the roots, imagine a line on the soil equal to the circumference of the foliage.

PLANTING PERENNIAL TRANSPLANTS

1 Dig a hole half again as wide and twice as deep as the nursery container of your perennial plant. Mix balanced fertilizer into the removed soil along with abundant organic compost.

Most perennial plants are sold in 1-gallon (4-l) or 5-gallon (20-l) nursery containers. Choose plants that have developed roots that fill their pots, but avoid those that are rootbound. Plants should be healthy and free of obvious insect infestation. Water transplants the day before placing them into the garden, then follow these easy steps to plant your perennials:

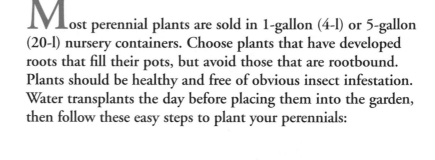

2 Invert the container and gently tap its bottom and sides to remove the plant. Let it slide gently into your outstretched hand.

3 With a hand fork, break up any encircling roots to ensure that the plant quickly establishes itself.

5 Immediately water the transplant to settle the soil and refresh the plant. Water frequently for the first ten days, then gradually reduce the frequency until the plant receives water about once a week or when the soil becomes dry.

4 Place the plant in the hole so that its container soil line is level with the surrounding soil. Backfill around the sides of the rootball and press the soil firmly against it.

PLANTING SHRUBS

A plant should be proportionate to the size of its contaier or it may be an indication that it is rootbound. Check the bottom of the container for signs of root growth through the drainage holes. A plant with proper root development will slide easily from its container.

Shrubs form part of your shade garden's "bones." They give structure to your landscaping and a framework for perennials, annuals, and ground covers. Some —such as azalea, camellia, and holly—can be focal points in your design as well.

Shrubs either are deciduous or evergreen. The latter are used mostly for their interesting foliage and as backdrop for other plants. Deciduous shrubs specialize in seasonal foliage and flowers. Within these categories are shrubs for dry shade, moist shade, and wet shade, in heights ranging from a foot (30 cm) to 10 feet (3 m). The taller varieties are most effective in woodland gardens and spacious shade areas. They also work well as hedging that creates a "wall" between a shade garden and other parts of the yard. Smaller varieties—the more compact hydrangeas, for example—are best in a proportionally sized shade garden.

Before buying a shrub, note its height and spread relative to its container. Buying the most mature-looking specimen on the lot may be tempting, but if the plant looks too big for the container, it may be rootbound. Once you are ready to plant your shrub, loosen it carefully from its container. If roots are tightly coiled around the rootball, gently spray it with a stream of water and carefully uncoil the roots.

Planting a shrub from a 1-gallon (4-l) or 5-gallon (20-l) nursery container is not unlike planting a tree. Since it will be in its spot for the long haul, place it well, allowing room for its expected size at maturity. For azaleas and camellias, lighten the composition of the backfill soil with organic amendments such as peat moss. Azaleas do well planted in pure peat, while camellias prefer a half-peat, half-soil mix. For other types of shrubs, mix some balanced fertilizer or super-phosphate into the bottom of the hole before planting.

Some of the favored deciduous shrubs for shade include rhododendrons; camellias, both japonica and sasanqua varieties; azaleas; hollies, which put out beautiful red berries in winter; witch hazels, which cover themselves with yellow blooms in autumn; and hydrangeas, which come in a variety of sizes. Among coniferous favorites are various yews, which deer won't touch, and Russian cypress. All make delightful additions to a shade garden family.

Low, mounding shrubs are a perfect foundation for interplantings of colorful annuals and foliage plants in a range of contrasting greens.

PLANTING SHRUBS IN SHADE

Most shrub planting follows a process similar to that used for other large plants and trees. For best results, dig a hole about twice the diameter and depth of the rootball. Amend the soil removed from the hole with an equal amount of compost and a balanced fertilizer. Partially refill the hole with the amended soil, until its depth is the same as the rootball of the plant. Then follow the instructions shown:

1 Large shrubs are heavy. Turn the container on its side, gently tap on the container walls to loosen the plant, and slide it out.

2 With a sharp trowel, score the rootball vertically to cut any encircling roots and force growth outward.

3 Place the rootball in the center of the hole. The container soil line should be the same as the planting soil surface. If the plant is set too low, remove it and add more fill; if too high, remove more soil.

4 When the shrub is correctly positioned, backfill around it with more amended soil. Create a moat around the plant to contain early watering and allow for settling of the soil.

5 Firm the soil around the rootball with your hands to ensure good soil contact.

PLANTING TREES

If you are like many shade gardeners, you are planting in shade cast by a large tree or trees on your property. If this is the case, the type of shade garden you plant will be influenced by the particular trees and their growth habits.

Set in a support stake after positioning the tree but before planting to avoid disturbing the tree roots. Loosely encircle the tree and stake with a support wire, reinforced with a rubber chafe protector to prevent damage to the tree.

On the other hand, if you are planning to plant trees with the purpose of creating fine shade in years to come or to plant understory—that is, smaller trees under an existing canopy of tall overstory trees—you have the opportunity to plant the perfect shade-producing trees as well as those adapted to shady situations. You can avoid problem trees that cast too much shade or ones with shallow roots that compete ruthlessly for water and nutrients. In other words, you can plant good neighbors for your shade garden to come.

If you intend to plant anywhere near the trees, avoid conifers. As beautiful as they appear in a park or woodland setting, these trees either cast so deep a shade that little will grow under them, or they are shallow-rooted and greedy gobblers of all available moisture and nutrients. Shallow-rooted trees also make soil cultivation tricky and often aggravating.

For your shade garden, select trees that grow to a mature height in scale with your yard, your house, and your neighborhood. Deciduous trees are better than evergreens since they allow winter and spring sun to bring understory plantings to life. It helps if their branches are loose limbed to move with wind and have leaves that are feathery and small to allow sunlight to filter through to the ground below. Roots should sink deep. If you are looking to plant smaller trees that will thrive in shade conditions under an existing canopy of tall trees, consider Japanese maple, Russian olive, and smaller magnolias.

Whichever trees you consider, know their full height and spread at maturity. Before you make the commitment to buy, mark off the ultimate spread on the ground using sand or chalk so you will see exactly how far your shade will extend.

If your patience level or needs inspire you to purchase a more mature tree, keep in mind that you probably will need help to plant it. Fertilize it heavily upon planting, and water it abundantly for the first three months in its new location.

PLANTING TREES IN SHADE GARDENS

Trees are available in bare root form, in 5- and 15-gallon (20- and 55-l) containers, and as boxed specimens. Plant smaller trees as you would shrubs [see Planting Shrubs in Shade, pg. 59]. Boxed specimens allow you to have instantaneous results, but there is a commensurate increase in effort that accompanies the task. Remember that soil and trees are unwieldy and heavy; avoid hazard from lifting by using a helper and proper lifting technique. Follow these steps for planting a large tree:

1 Locate the tree at the site and lower it to a horizontal position. With a hatchet, remove the bottom of the box to free the roots.

2 Leaving the sides of the box in place, remove the bottom binder strap. Prepare a hole one-third wider and deeper than the box. Add a balanced starter fertilizer. Using care, lower the tree into the hole, break the final binder, and remove the sides from the tree's rootball.

3 Backfill around the rootball of the tree using soil from the hole mixed with an equal part of compost. Compact the soil as you fill to ensure there are no air pockets.

4 Water the tree to refresh it and settle the soil. If slumping occurs, add more fill. The soil line of the tree should be 1–2 in. (25–50 mm) higher than the surrounding soil.

PLANTING FERNS

Descended from some of the oldest plants on earth, ferns do not propagate by producing flowers as do most plants. Instead, they produce spores—which often appear as dark-brown welts on the undersides of their fronds—which dry up and drop off to produce young ferns. Despite the delicacy of their appearance, most ferns are hardy survivors. Not surprisingly, there are ferns for almost every soil and moisture condition. Most, however, prefer an exceptionally loose, moist soil that is humus-rich and they are best planted in light to open shade. They will grow in rock crevices, on slopes as well as flat ground, and in containers.

Ferns are among the easiest shade plants to grow if you keep in mind that they are adapted to moist, leafy forest floors where their rhizomes can run just under the soil surface. Plant ferns in the spring or autumn in an area that mimics, as closely as possible, their native forest conditions. This likely means you will have to amend your soil. Rake up any fallen leaves, then work into the soil some dampened peat moss and a fair amount of leaf mold or organic compost. Dig a hole deeper by half than the fern rootball you're planting, then dig 4–6 inches (10–15 cm) around the hole to allow for root growth. Some dry superphosphate worked into the bottom of the hole will give the fern an initial boost.

(Top) Dig a hole deeper and wider by half than the fern rootball you're planting to allow for new growth. (Above) To retain soil moisture, mulch with bark chips or other organic mulch.

Plant the fern so that the juncture between root and stem does not fall below ground level. To do this, initially place the fern 5 inches (13 cm) above ground level, since the amended soil will settle after watering. Tamp the soil gently to firm the plant in the hole, but avoid compacting the soil too much, either by intent or by walking. Scatter bark chips or organic mulch to finish the bed.

If the site lacks moisture, consider supplementing it with an irrigation system [see opposite]. Drip systems are particularly effective for keeping the soil floor moist. If your area is prone to dry winds or is very humid, think about installing a sprayer/mister to keep plants hydrated.

Ferns are among the easiest shade plants to grow and maintain. If soil is well prepared and mulch is regularly applied, they require little other maintenance than clipping off dried fronds with pruning shears.

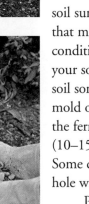

WATERING FERNS

Ferns vary tremendously in their need for moisture. Some prefer constantly damp soil, while others are adapted to periodic waterings followed by near drought. If your shady site lacks natural moisture, supplement it with an artificial irrigation source by adding a drip system [see A Simple Drip System, pg. 49]. Such systems permit you to tailor irrigation on a plant-by-plant basis. Follow these steps once the system lines have been extended to the shade garden:

1 Using proper fittings for your system, attach the lateral tubing to the main supply line and extend to the fern.

2 Drip emitters may be placed at ground level to soak the roots or suspended on stakes to mist the fern's foliage.

3 Attach the emitter to the supply tube by pressing the fitting together. to create a leak-proof junction.

4 For moisture-loving ferns, choose a sprayer head and suspend it well above the fern's top foliage by mounting it on a plastic stake.

5 Turn the system on and adjust the spray to dampen foliage and soak the ground around each fern plant.

BULBS IN A SHADE GARDEN

It may be surprising that shade gardens can be hospitable to flowering bulbs, corms, and tubers, since bulbs generally prefer slightly moist and well-drained soil to that of wet woodlands. Too much water means almost certain death by fungal disease for most bulbs. However, an open, shaded location that doesn't become boggy in rain can work well, especially if the bulbs are spring flowering and repose under a canopy of deciduous trees.

Spring bulbs well-suited to shade include tiny blue Siberian squill, checkered fritillaria, glory-of-the-snow, snowdrops, green-dotted spring snowflake, a slew of cheery daffodils, narcissus, jonquils, crocus, tulips, purplish grape hyacinth, and bell-like wood hyacinth. Summer flowering bulbs for shade include pendulous tuberous begonias, cyclamen, a host of lilies, freesias, and caladiums, which are prized for their colorful foliage. While these bulbs can be planted in formal patterns in the shade bed, they look their best when "naturalized," or scattered roughly across the soil to create irregular drifts of flowers. This works splendidly, as you can imagine, in a woodsy shade garden, but the effect also can be achieved in a shade bed under a large tree.

Different planting depths suit different bulbs. For a cluster of the same type of bulb, you can save time by digging the entire area to the desired depth. Bulbs need potassium and phosphorus. Work dry, granular, slow-release fertilizers, such as bulb boosters, into 2 or 3 inches (5 or 8 cm) of soil at the bottom of the bed, then lighten the soil you've removed by adding organic matter such as leaf mold. Scatter your bulbs gently across the prepared bed and set them firmly, root side down, where they land. Fill the bed with the amended soil, tamp down lightly, and water in well. Water only when the soil surface seems dry, and avoid watering at all if you get regular rain.

After the flush of flowers is gone, it's tempting to cut back the bulbs' scraggly foliage, but resist that temptation. Bulbs gain their strength to flower again the following year through their foliage. Fertilize again, carefully digging more bulb booster around the plants and cut back the foliage only when it has yellowed and withered. To minimize the unsightliness, overplant the bulbs with low-growing, shallow-rooted annuals.

For a "naturalized" look, plant bulbs by scattering them randomly across the prepared bed to create irregular drifts. For a more formal look, plant individual bulbs in prepared holes set at regular intervals.

PLANTING BULBS

Prepare the bed as you would for annuals—double dig, amend with abundant organic compost, and lightly fertilize. In cold-winter climates, plant hardy bulbs in autumn and allow them to rest over winter. In mild-winter climates, chill bulbs 4–6 weeks in the refrigerator before setting them out in spring. Follow these simple steps to plant most bulbs, corms, and tubers:

1 Use a dibber or bulb planter to create a hole twice the bulb's diameter and 4–6 in. (10–15 cm) deep.

2 Place the bulb in the excavated hole, with its base down, not more than 1 in. (25 mm) beneath the soil surface. If necessary, backfill the hole before placing the bulb in it.

3 Fill the hole with a mixture of loose compost and native soil. Press soil firmly.

DIGGING, DIVIDING, AND STORING BULBS

Some bulbs, such as daffodils and crocus, "naturalize" into their settings, which means they propagate and spread and can be left in the same position from year to year. Other bulbs, such as lilies, and tender corms, such as tuberous begonias, do better if you dig them up, let them dry a few days, carefully shake off all excess soil from between the roots, divide them, pack them gently and loosely in moist sawdust or peat moss, and store them in a cool, dry place. Do this after the foliage has yellowed and withered but before it has fallen off or you will have a tough time finding the bulbs. Bulbs develop tiny bulb offshoots that should be separated from the main bulb before planting the next year.

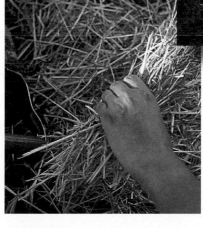

4 If winters are severe in your area, mulch the bed with a heavy layer of straw to insulate it from snow and ice.

H ow you care for your shade plants after they are in the ground and how good an eye you develop for spotting problems early are as important as proper soil preparation and appropriate climate conditions. In the following pages, we cover all the maintenance basics—watering, fertilizing, pruning, and pest and disease control.

The importance of proper watering in shade conditions may be even greater than it is for sunny gardens. Too much water can drown or rot many shade plants, while too little can quickly desiccate moisture-loving plants. The range of hand-operated and timer-driven irrigation systems available today makes responding to different shade-garden watering needs much easier. While fertilizing generally is less necessary in a properly prepared shade garden than in a sunny one, some fertilizing can boost plants, particularly acid-loving azaleas and gardenias. We provide insight into the proper way to apply different types of fertilizers, from foliar to liquid to solid organic forms.

> **Good watering, fertilizing, and pruning will ensure a shade garden nearly free of pests and disease**

Caring for Shade Plants

Pruning, pinching, and clipping are as critical to keeping your garden in top condition as watering and fertilizing. You'll read about how to keep your garden looking its best throughout the growing season.

Finally, you'll find out how to spot the pests, fungi, and diseases that can decimate even the most carefully prepared garden. We provide well-measured advice on your options for dealing with common shade-garden pests, including discussions on pesticidal and non-pesticidal soaps and environment-friendly pest-control treatments. We'll also let you know how to spot the signs of problems early on, how to salvage plants, and how to evaluate whether to treat a plant or remove it.

Since most shade gardens are created to last, these tips can ensure that yours will grow and thrive for years to come.

Proper watering is arguably the single most important aspect of maintaining a healthy shade garden. Too much water can promote fungal disease and too little can seriously compromise moisture-loving plants.

WATERING NEEDS

One of the wonderful features of a shade garden is how little water it requires relative to other gardens. As you would imagine, water evaporates at a much slower rate in a shade garden than in a sunny one, and falling leaves from overhead trees, properly composted, often act as water-retentive mulch.

Hoses can be outfitted with a number of different nozzles to provide fine to coarse sprays; they also can be equipped with long-handled wands perfect for direct application of water to an area and for watering hanging plants.

Of course, some shade plants need more water than others. Trying to strike a compromise between dry-shade lovers and moist-shade lovers will suit neither, so group your shade plantings according to their watering needs as well as their light requirements. Remember that shade plants will compete with any nearby shallow-rooted trees for water, so check the moisture level of the soil frequently.

Because shade gardens tend to have higher moisture levels than other types of gardens, check the soil before you water by digging down 4–5 inches (10–13 cm). If the soil is still damp, delay watering. Too much water terminates root growth and cuts off oxygen, allowing root rot to set in. The only exception is moisture-loving plants suited to tropical conditions where abundant rainfall isn't a problem. These plantings actually benefit from regular misting. For shade plants that prefer slightly moist or dry conditions, water infrequently but deeply to encourage root growth.

Several methods are effective for watering shade gardens. If your shade garden is small, watering by hand with a watering can or hose may be the most beneficial. Watering cans and hose-end sprayers can be fitted with fine-holed nozzles to deliver water gently. Hoses also can be outfitted with long-handled wands for container plantings. High-humidity plants benefit from a misting system that humidifies the entire setting. Other watering systems include in-ground irrigation [see In-ground Irrigation Systems, pg. 46] and simple drip systems [see Drip Irrigation Systems, pg. 48]. Evaluate your shade garden's needs to determine which system is best for you.

(Left) A drip emitter delivers water slowly and reliably; it can be equipped with a sensor that monitors soil moisture, then waters whenever the plant needs irrigation. (Right) A watering can with a fine-holed nozzle, or "rose," is perfect for gentle watering of delicate plants in a small-space garden.

If your soil is well prepared from the start, the fertilization needs of your shade garden will be relatively simple. Plants need a little more than a dozen nutrients—some, which usually are present in soil, in trace amounts and others that rarely are found in natural soil in sufficient amounts.

FERTILIZING NEEDS

Plants get their needed carbon, hydrogen, and oxygen from the air and water. To thrive, they also need a certain amount of calcium, manganese, zinc, calcium, sulfur, and iron, all of which are found in most soils. The three essential elements plants need are nitrogen, phosphorus, and potassium.

For most shade plantings, an all-purpose fertilizer scattered across the soil bed or incorporated into the bottom of holes before planting will be sufficient, but check the Encyclopedia of Shade Plants [see pg. 79] for the specific needs of the plants you've chosen. Fertilizing is made much simpler if plant varieties with similar needs are grouped together.

A number of fertilizers are water soluble, and some, such as liquid fish emulsion, must be diluted before application. In general, they are used as plant boosters.

Some fertilizers can be applied dry to the soil surface, worked in gently with a hand fork, then watered in thoroughly. Other dry or semi-dry fertilizers are water soluble and must be dissolved before application. These fertilizers are absorbed through foliage as well as roots, so carefully pour or spray them with a hose-end applicator over the entire plant early in the day. Liquid fertilizers, such as fish emulsion, also need to be diluted and should be poured around your plants.

Fertilizers are available in organic and inorganic, natural and synthetic, fast-acting and slow-release types. Choose the one that fits your needs and gardening practices while providing adequate nutrition to your plants. Slow-acting, organic fertilizers take some time to break down into usable nutrients but generally are excellent for building good soil. Fast-acting fertilizers provide quick results but must be used carefully because they can burn leaves if overapplied.

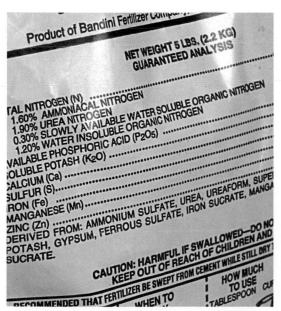

(Left) Before choosing a fertilizer, carefully read the entire package label and match the fertilizer to the needs of both your soil and the plants you have chosen.

(Right) Water-soluble fertilizers are absorbed through leaves as well as roots, making them quick acting.

PRUNING

Pruning remains one of the most underappreciated garden tasks, yet few things are more important to the development of a garden. Among the many reasons to prune, health is primary. Cutting off dead foliage and broken branches discourages pests and eliminates entry points for disease. Appearance is another. An unkempt plant, with broken and crossed branches and unruly growth patterns, destroys any harmony in a bed or border; however, a well-pruned plant doesn't appear to have been pruned at all; it seems naturally clean, healthy, and elegant. Pruning also promotes spreading, creating a shapely mounding plant instead of a spindly tall one. Thriving flower production is yet another reason to prune. Deadheading, or cutting off flowers past their prime, encourages a plant, annuals in particular, to produce more flowers. Finally, pruning trees protects your property and yourself from the hazard of falling branches.

There are many ways to prune: different types of plants require different techniques. The simplest method is pinching [see left]. Pinching helps encourage side growth, giving the plant a pleasing, well-rounded shape. Annuals and some perennials only require pinching, and the earlier in the plant's growth cycle you begin providing care by pinch pruning, the better.

Heading [see Pruning Shrubs, pg. 72] consists of removing the terminal growth and part of the shoot back to a latent bud further down the branch or stem. Heading results in vigorous new growth from the bud below the cut, which can revitalize straggly shrubs. Shearing is the process of shaping a plant, such as squaring a hedge or rounding a conifer, and mainly is reserved for creating topiaries and shaping formal garden hedges. Thinning is the art of removing lesser branches back to the trunk, to increase air circulation and promote more vigorous growth and flower production on the remaining branches.

Deciduous trees are best pruned in autumn or late winter, before they begin to develop spring growth, so that the tree's energy will be directed to the remaining branches [see opposite]. Evergreens rarely need pruning because their growth is compact, but you can trim them as needed for appearance.

1 Pinch pruning is the simplest form of plant care. Use it to "deadhead" spent blossoms and to remove leggy foliage. Annual flowers will stop blooming if dead blossoms are allowed to go to seed. Remove them to prolong the bloom.

2 Locate the junction with the stalk of the flower stem to be removed. Using your thumbnail and index finger, pinch off the stem. Repeat for each spent flower or leggy stem of foliage.

3 After the plant has been pinch pruned it will begin another blooming cycle and new growth will make the plant appear more compact and full.

USING A POLE PRUNER

Large deciduous trees benefit from regular prunings, as do the plantings beneath them. Pruning removes dead or diseased wood, eliminates tangled branches, reduces the overall size of the canopy, shapes the tree, and allows more light to reach its trunk and interior branches. A telescoping pole pruning tool is essential for tall foliage and branch removal. Exercise caution and always wear eye protection and safety equipment when using a pole pruner, following these steps:

2 Loosen the knurled nut and extend the telescoping pole to slightly more than the height of the limbs to be pruned.

1 Loosen the retaining ring, extend the telescoping pole, and tighten until locked. Check that the rope pull assembly is free and operating properly.

3 The shear jaws are meant for branches of 2 in. (5 cm) in diameter or less. Place the jaws around a limb and pull on the rope to cleanly cut through the wood.

4 Use the pruning saw to cut large branches first from the underside, then from the top. Take extra care to avoid bark tears and hazard from falling branches.

PRUNING SHRUBS

Periodic pruning of shrubs invigorates their growth, shapes them, and keeps them free of disease. Most woody shrubs can be pruned with hand pruners, either a bypass or anvil model. Prune blooming shrubs after their flowers have dropped; prune other deciduous shrubs and evergreens annually in the autumn. Follow the steps shown:

1 Before beginning major pruning, remove any lateral branches that extend from the margins of the shrub. Cut them just above a leaf or latent bud.

2 Annual spikes grow from the top of many woody shrubs. Remove them 4–6 in. (10–15 cm) below the margin of the shrub formed by the prior year's growth.

3 Major pruning is required when the shrub has become leggy, has dead branches, or has shoots that cross the center line.

4 Reach into the center of the shrub and prune away crossing branches at their junction with a main branch or trunk.

5 Remove weak and spindly branches; preserve hardy, vigorous growth. Usually 3–4 branches will remain.

6 After pruning, the shrub should exhibit a classic vase shape and all areas of its foliage should receive good light and air.

CONTROLLING PESTS

The use of pesticides remains the most controversial aspect of home gardening, but intervention sometimes is necessary to control infestation or disease. After all of your hard work and effort in creating a lush shade garden, it is difficult, indeed, to watch it being devoured by pests. Shade gardens, unfortunately, feature just the type of dark, moist environment that is paradise to snails, slugs, black vine and root weevils, and earwigs. Hostas particularly are prey to slugs and snails, which can turn those beautiful broad leaves into Swiss cheese, seemingly overnight. It's little wonder many people turn to potent pesticides, but it's important to realize that using chemical controls can be a mistake, especially as a first defense.

Pesticides are effective killers, no doubt. The trouble is, they are not discriminatory. They also kill beneficial subsurface microbial life, earthworms, and other helpful bugs and insects along with their targets. After use, you might start noticing, for instance, that there are fewer, or no, honeybees to pollinate your fruit trees or vegetables. Out of sight, toxic chemicals leach far down into the soil and aquifer to reach the groundwater that leads to your water supply; are carried in rainwater and sprinkler runoff into the streets and sewers where they are dumped into the ocean; and are eaten in the form of poisoned bugs by birds and other animals that deposit the residues as waste here, there, and everywhere. There comes a point when you need to decide if you're willing to pay such a price for "perfection."

As readily available as these chemicals are, remember at all times that they are hazardous. The "active"—or toxic—ingredient will be listed on the product label as a percentage by weight, along with the specific pests for which it is deemed effective, and complete instructions for use.

Here's the good news: there are alternatives to pesticides. The principles of organic and integrated pest

(Left) Because of their moist conditions, many shade gardens are paradise to a number of pests. (Above) A number of botanical insecticides use environment-friendly coumpounds derived from plants. Still, apply them with care, taking all necessary precautions advised on their labels.

Before each and every use of an insecticide, read the product label carefully and follow its directions to the letter. Protect your hands with gloves, your eyes with goggles, and use a respirator. Never apply pesticides or other garden chemicals when it is windy, and restrict access to treated areas by children and pets until any hazard to health has passed.

management (IPM) were developed for agricultural concerns, but they apply equally to home gardening. IPM is based on the premise that pests should be managed, not eradicated entirely. This means that you trade off a certain amount of plant loss to pests to ensure that the micro- and macro-environments are preserved. You can attack the pests, but the idea is to use the tools of nature and its system of checks and balances to combat your garden foes. IPM assumes that the least toxic control methods will be used first, followed by increased efforts with stronger controls when the infestation or infection is resistant.

The first goal is to maintain a healthy plant environment. Healthy plants most often can fend for and defend themselves. A second tool is to use nature's own weapons against pest malefactors. Lacewings, for example, are insects that feed on a variety of destructive insects and mites. Certain non-pesticidal soap solutions containing sodium or potassium salts combined with oil are time-honored forms of non-toxic pesticides that affect soft-bodied pests such as aphids, mealybugs, whiteflies, and the like. They are generally harmless to the user and remain in the soil for a very short time [see opposite]. The drawbacks of soaps are that they must be applied directly to the pests and reapplied often; they also are harmful to bees. Experts recommend their use in spring, when pests are multiplying rapidly, either very early in the morning or late at night, when bees are in their hives.

Controlling snails and slugs is more difficult, since they eat at night and hide during the day. One way to nab the culprits is to take a flashlight and empty coffee can out to the garden after dark. Hand pick the slugs and put them in the can, secure the lid tightly, and throw it into the trash. Another method is to sprinkle a protective barrier of diatomaceous earth, a white powder made from ground fossilized skeletons of tiny sea creatures, which snails and slugs won't cross.

Whichever methods of eradication you choose, make an informed choice for yourself, your family, and your environment.

Slugs and snails can be particularly elusive prey. Hand picking is the most reliable—and environment-friendly—method. Take a trusty flashlight out at night, place the pests in a coffee can, secure the lid, and dispose of the can. Another method is to prop a plank between two rocks. Snails and slugs will attach themselves to the underside; the next morning, simply turn over the plank, pluck off the pests, place them in a sealable container, and dispose of them in the trash.

APPLYING INSECTICIDAL SOAP

Insecticidal soaps are a good approach to treating early infestations of plant pests. To be effective, the soap solution must be applied directly to the pest causing damage. Remember to treat the undersides of leaves, where most pests live. Although insecticidal soaps are minimally toxic to humans, always follow label instructions carefully and completely. Mix and apply the soap solution following the steps shown:

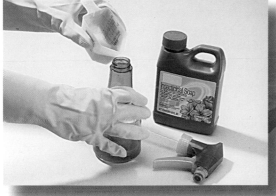

2 Apply the insecticidal soap directly to the insect pests, making sure to spray both the tops and bottoms of the leaves as well as any infested stems.

1 Following all package instructions and wearing protective gloves, mix the soap solution in a misting hand sprayer.

APPLYING SYSTEMIC PESTICIDE

Systemic pesticides are absorbed by the plant along with water and nutrients, making their sap toxic to insects. Use only systemic pesticides labeled as appropriate for the type of plant.

1 Measure granular systemic pesticide carefully, following the dose instructions on the product label.

2 Evenly sprinkle the pesticide granules onto the soil in a circle, beneath the outermost foliage of the plant.

3 Using a hand fork, work the granules into the soil to prevent hazard to pets and to ensure good absorption.

CONTROLLING FUNGI AND DISEASES

Failure to keep seedlings warm enough during germination may result in "damping off," a fungal disease evidenced by a brown ring around the stem just above the soil and general plant failure. Closely adhere to the recommended soil temperatures for your chosen plants.

Shade plants, by nature of their preferred environment, are particularly prone to disease, especially fungal diseases. Like humans, plants are susceptible to bacterial and viral infections as well. You can spot a viral disease in a plant quickly. Affected plants are strangely shaped and stunted, and their color patterns are oddly broken or mottled. There are no cures for virus-infected plants. Your sole recourse is to remove the infected plant before the virus spreads and either burn it or dispose of it in the trash. Do not compost an infected plant or you risk spreading the virus. Replace the plant with a virus-resistant variety.

Plants also can be attacked by various fungi, which are spread by spores carried from plant to plant by wind or water. Among the most common for shade areas are powdery mildew, black spot, rust, root rot, and water mold. There are fungicides to treat these problems [see opposite], but they are toxic chemicals that are long lasting in the soil, so use them in a limited fashion. Fertilize and cultivate diseased plants to restore their vigor.

Fungal-diseased plants often can be brought back to health, but they should be isolated from healthy plants. You can accomplish this in several ways. Leave the plant where it is and surround it with wooden stakes linked together with wire and wrapped in clear plastic. Trim off the diseased leaves and stems, carefully removing them to prevent the spread of spores, then burn them or dispose of them in the trash and disinfect your shears. Better yet, gently remove the plant and replant it in a warmer, drier, and lighter spot. Mildew and rust in particular react unfavorably to hot, dry conditions. Finally, consider digging out 4–6 inches (10–15 cm) of soil surrounding the infected plant and replacing it with fresh soil. Spores wash down into the upper soil level where splashes of water send them back up onto leaves to propagate anew. For a fungus such as root rot, which can be caused by too much water coupled with poor drainage, amend the soil to improve drainage and reduce watering to the area until the disease subsides.

When dealing with fungal infections in particular, look beyond the diseased plant to the environment that fostered the disease. Well-drained soil and adequate air circulation limit fungal growth; improving soil drainage and increasing air flow in your garden are your most important steps toward preventing future problems.

Fungal-diseased plants often can be brought back to health, but they must be isolated from neighboring plants. Wrap the plant in plastic after treatment.

APPLYING FUNGICIDE

Fungal diseases are among the most common disease problems encountered in shade gardens. If pruning to improve air flow in the garden is not sufficient, consider application of a fungicidal control to the affected area. Remember that fungicides are potent chemicals with health hazards to you and the environment, so always follow the package label instructions exactly. Use these steps to treat an infection caused by mold, mildew, black spot, or other fungi:

1 Select a fungicide that specifically lists the disease you wish to treat, read its label carefully, and follow all instructions for mixing the control. A hose-end sprayer is ideal for widespread infections.

2 If the sprayer has an adjustable flow setting, set it to the desired rate. Fixed-rate sprayers require users to dilute the concentrated fungicide before filling the sprayer. Apply the control agent to the infected area. Be sure to include the undersides of leaves, stems, and the soil beneath the plant. Always spray on windless mornings, allowing sufficent time for the foliage to dry before nightfall. Wear protective clothing, gloves, eye protection, and a respirator.

3 After application, wash the sprayer to clean it. Discard unused concentrate safely.

A

ll the preparation in the world won't help a poorly chosen plant thrive in your shade garden. This may seem like an obvious point, but who of us has not been mesmerized by a garden catalog or overtaken by shopping frenzy at the local nursery? A good dose, or even an overdose, of optimism is generally a good thing in a person, but it can be an expensive quality in a gardener.

Fortunately, this book contains a comprehensive encyclopedia of shade plants that describes in detail the type of soil, moisture, and lighting requirements for an abundance of plants, including their preferred climate zones. If a plant craves acid soil and yours is generally alkaline, you will have to either amend it or plant in a raised bed. Almost certainly, if you plunk a plant down in poorly matched soil, it will be a loss. Likewise, you may adore peonies but if you live in Southern California where winter temperatures rarely dip below 40°F (4°C), this is not a good fit, and it's better to know before rather than after you've paid for the shipping and handling.

> **Nearly 100 plant varieties at your fingertips, with all the necessary pictures and facts to create great shade gardens**

Encyclopedia of Shade Plants

Light conditions also are critical. A plant that receives less light than it needs will grow low and spindly and may not flower at all. In addition, plants that can grow in part shade, meaning some full sun during the day, are different creatures than those requiring medium or filtered shade all day. The latter can scorch with direct light, on its leaves and flowers while the former may not flower without direct sun.

If you see a plant that you think you can't live without, but it requires more sun than your area offers, take heart. There's always an acceptable counterpart in the diverse world of shade plants. If you can't grow delphiniums, you can grow splendid foxgloves. Petunias need sun, but colorful impatiens need shade. Accommodating azaleas come in varieties for shade as well as for sun. Finally, don't forget about the many virtues of moveable containers, which allow you to create the shade garden look, even if it's for only part of the day.

Shade is a welcome addition to warm-sun areas, such as patios and swimming-pool decks. A shade structure permits both climbing vines and hanging plants to provide cool relief from the sun's glare.

ANNUALS

Common name: Alyssum, Sweet
Scientific name: *Lobularia maritima*
Description: ¾-in. (20-mm) fragrant flower clusters in white, lilac, pink, or purple. Leaves are narrow and green. Multibranched plant grows to less than 1 ft. (30 cm) tall.
Plant hardiness: Zones 2–10.
Soil needs: Moist, well-drained soil. Fertility: average. Overfeeding this plant will lead to an abundance of foliage at the expense of flowers. Neutral 7.0 pH.
Shade degree: Partial shade.
Watering requirement: Water regularly.
Spacing of plants: 6 in. (15 cm) apart.
Tips and care: If plant seems to be wilting in midsummer, cut back foliage; when climate cools, it will bounce back with more blooms. Also, deadhead to promote further flowering. A favorite for edging. Works well in a rock garden. Attracts bees.

The budding twigs spread out their fan
To catch the breezy air;
And I must think, do all I can,
That there was pleasure there.

WILLIAM WORDSWORTH

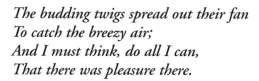

Common name: Begonia, Wax
Scientific name: *Begonia* × *semperflorens-cultorum*
Description: 1-in.-wide (25-mm) waxy flowers are white, pink, or red covering small mounds of bronze-green foliage. The plant grows 8–12 in. (20–30 cm) tall.
Plant hardiness: Zones 2–10.
Soil needs: Well-drained loamy soil. Fertility: rich. Supplement with peat moss, compost, or leaf mold. Neutral 7.0 pH.
Shade degree: Partial to moderate shade.
Watering requirement: Water frequently.
Spacing of plants: 8–10 in. (20–25 cm) apart.
Tips and care: Watch out for whiteflies, mealybugs, and leaf spot. Works well in shaded windowboxes, hanging baskets, and borders. Not very cold hardy.

Common name: Black-eyed Susan
Scientific name: *Rudbeckia hirta*
Description: 2–6-in.-wide (5–15-cm) yellow, gold, red, or mahogany flowers with dark-brown or bright-green centers. Leaves are rough, hairy, and dark green. Plant grows 1–3 ft. (30–90 cm) tall and about 2 ft. (60 cm) wide.
Plant hardiness: Zones 3–10.
Soil needs: Loamy, moist, well-drained soil. Fertility: average. Tolerates poor soils. Neutral 7.0 pH.
Shade degree: Partial to light shade.
Watering requirement: Water regularly.
Spacing of plants: 1–2 ft. (30–60 cm) apart.
Tips and care: Nice massed in beds, borders, and meadow plantings. Good cutting flower—immerse cut stems in boiling water before arranging.

Common name: Butterfly Flower
Scientific name: *Schizanthus* x *wisetonensis*
Description: Orchidlike clusters of flowers in white, blue, pink, yellow, red, magenta, or multicolored with a streaked-yellow upper lip atop strong stems. Plant grows 1–2 ft. (30–60 cm) tall and about 1 ft. (30 cm) wide.
Plant hardiness: Zones 3–9.
Soil needs: Moist, loose, well-drained loamy soil. Fertility: rich. Supplement with organic matter. Neutral 7.0 pH.
Shade degree: Partial to light shade.
Watering requirement: Water moderately; keep soil moist.
Spacing of plants: 12 in. (30 cm) apart.
Tips and care: Good in massed beds, edgings, borders, and containers. Good cutting flower. Sow more seeds every couple of weeks in mild-winter climates.

Common name: Canterbury Bells
Scientific name: *Campanula medium*
Description: 2-in.-long (50-mm) and 1-in.-wide (25-mm) bell-shaped violet-blue flowers bloom off 2–3-ft.-tall (60–90 cm) stems.
Plant hardiness: Zones 3–8.
Soil needs: Moist, well-drained soil. Fertility: rich. Neutral to alkaline 7.0–7.5 pH.
Shade degree: Partial to light shade.
Watering requirement: Water moderately.
Spacing of plants: 12 in. (30 cm) apart.
Tips and care: Susceptible to pests and diseases; destroy infected plants. Good cutting flower. Nice in borders and meadow plantings. Pinch off faded flowers to keep plant vigorous and attractive.

COLEUS

Anyone who thinks a shade garden cannot match a sun garden for brilliant color has never seen coleus in action. Coleus, known also as flame nettle, are prized for their outrageous, brazen foliage. Leaves generally feature more than one color, and sometimes three, in a dizzying number of combinations, including pinks, mauve, maroon, gold, orange, red, greens, chartreuse, burgundy, and cream. Grown as an annual, coleus's foliage is so desirable that gardeners usually pluck off the rather pallid flower spikes before they blossom to keep the plant bushy and full. Hardy to zone 11, coleus will grow wherever summers are warm and will adapt to light, medium, or even deeper shade, as long as they are planted in well-drained, humus-rich soil that is kept moist. In the right conditions, coleus will bush out to 3 feet (120 cm) tall by 3 feet (120 cm) wide.

Coleus, a member of the mint family, are best planted with ferns and other solid-green- or bronze-leafed shade plants, which bring out their strong color patterning. A bed or border planted solely with a variety of coleus, however, is a true summer eyepopper.

Coleus are among the easiest annuals to plant. They grow readily from seed after the last frost or can be started indoors eight to ten weeks earlier. They also root easily so you can ensure an offspring of a favorite for next year by clipping off a branch tip and placing it in water at summer's end. In a few weeks, pot the plant, then root clippings from this plant in late spring for transplanting outdoors.

Coleus foliage can be broad, smooth, toothed, scalloped, or fringed. Some standouts include the 'Saber' series, which has been bred to delay flowering, and 'Wizard,' which stays bushy throughout the summer.

Common name: Coleus, Garden
Scientific name: *Coleus hybridus*
Description: Foliage with fringed, scalloped, or toothy leaves grows to 3 ft. (90 cm) tall. Leaf colors in combinations of green, bronze, cream, pink, red, or maroon. Flowers are insignificant.
Plant hardiness: Zones 2–11.
Soil needs: Moist, well-drained soil. Fertility: rich. Feed occasionally during summer. Neutral to alkaline 7.0–7.5 pH.
Shade degree: Partial to full shade.
Watering requirement: Water regularly; keep soil moist.
Spacing of plants: 10–12 in. (25–30 cm) apart.
Tips and care: Beautiful in containers and borders. Pinch out flower stalks as they develop to promote compact foliage growth. Watch out for slugs and snails.

Common name: Cosmos

Scientific name: *Cosmos bipinnatus*

Description: 3–6-in.-wide (8–15-cm) daisylike flowers in white, pink, red, or lavender with yellow centers that bloom from long, thin stems. Leaves are bright green and lacy. Plant grows 3–4 ft. (90–120 cm) tall but can grow taller.

Plant hardiness: Zones 2–11.

Soil needs: Well drained to dry soil. Fertility: poor to average. Neutral to alkaline 7.0–7.5 pH.

Shade degree: Partial to light shade.

Watering requirement: Infrequent and light watering, drought tolerant.

Spacing of plants: 12 in. (30 cm) apart.

Tips and care: Heat tolerant. Resists pests and disease. Nice cutting flower.

Common name: Cupflower

Scientific name: *Nierembergia hippomanica*

Description: ¼-in. (6-mm) mounds of flowers in purple or violet with a yellow throat. Leaves are fine and fernlike. Plant grows to 12 in. (30 cm) tall and 12 in. (30 cm) wide.

Plant hardiness: Zones 2–10.

Soil needs: Moist, well-drained soil. Fertility: rich. Neutral 7.0 pH.

Shade degree: Partial to light shade.

Watering requirement: Water regularly; keep soil moist.

Spacing of plants: 6 in. (15 cm) apart.

Tips and care: Cut back after season's flowering to encourage compact growth for following season. Good for hanging baskets, edgings, and borders. Generally resistant to pests and diseases.

Common name: Feverfew

Scientific name: *Chrysanthemum parthenium*

Description: ¾-in. (20-mm) pillowlike flowers with yellow centers and short, ruffled petals. Stems are rounded and leafy.

Plant hardiness: Zones 5–10.

Soil needs: Moist, well-drained soil. Fertility: moderately rich. Supplement with compost or manure.

Shade degree: Partial shade.

Watering requirement: Water frequently.

Spacing of plants: 1–2 ft. (30–60 cm) apart.

Tips and care: Maintain plant's cushiony appearance by pinching back during summer growth. Good cutting flower; does well in hanging baskets and containers, rock gardens, and as a ground cover.

Common name: Five-Spot
Scientific name: *Nemophila maculata*
Description: Clusters of saucer-shaped flowers that are white with blue or purple tips. Plant grows in a low spreading manner 6–12 in. (15–30 cm) tall and 1 ft. (30 cm) wide.
Plant hardiness: Zones 7–9.
Soil needs: Sandy, well-drained soil. Fertility: average. Tolerates poor soil. Acid to alkaline 6.0–7.5 pH.
Shade degree: Partial shade.
Watering requirement: Keep soil moist during dry spells.
Spacing of plants: 9–12 in. (23–30 cm) apart.
Tips and care: Suited to coniferous forests and high altitudes; naturalizes in a wildflower landscape and along roadsides. Nice ground cover to accompany spring bulbs. Excellent for hanging baskets and rock gardens.

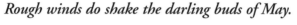

Rough winds do shake the darling buds of May.

WILLIAM SHAKESPEARE

Common name: Flossflower
Scientific name: *Ageratum houstonianum*
Description: ¼-in.-wide (6-mm) feathery, deep-blue flowers that grow in a mounded-shaped plant with leaves that are oval and glossy and have scalloped edges. Plant grows to about 14 in. (36 cm) tall.
Plant hardiness: Zones 2–10.
Soil needs: Sandy, well-drained soil. Fertility: rich. Neutral 7.0 pH.
Shade degree: Partial to light shade.
Watering requirement: Water regularly.
Spacing of plants: 6–9 in. (15–23 cm) apart.
Tips and care: Good cutting flower. Works well for edging. Blooming period from early summer to autumn.

Common name: Forget-Me-Not, Garden

Scientific name: *Myosotis sylvatica*

Description: 1/4-in. (6–mm) blue, pink, or white flowers with yellow centers bloom in clusters atop 1/4-in. (6-mm) slender stems. Mound-shaped plant grows 6–24 in. (15–60 cm) tall.

Plant hardiness: Zones 5–8.

Soil needs: Moist, well-drained soil. Fertility: moderately rich. Enrich with organic matter. Neutral 7.0 pH.

Shade degree: Partial to full shade.

Watering requirement: Water during dry periods; keep soil slightly moist.

Spacing of plants: 6–8 in. (15–20 cm) apart.

Tips and care: Good in edgings, beds, borders, rock gardens, and around bulbs.

A violet by the mossy stone
Half hidden from the eye!
Fair as a star when only one
Is shining in the sky.

WILLIAM WORDSWORTH

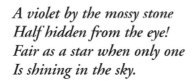

Common name: Geranium, Common

Scientific name: *Pelargonium* x *hortorum*

Description: 2–2 1/2-in.-wide (50–60-mm) rounded clusters of flowers in red, pink, white, coral, peach, orange, or bicolored. Leaves are 3–5 in. (8–13 cm) wide and sometimes contain a zone of dark color within the green. Plant grows 1–3 ft. (30–90 cm) tall.

Plant hardiness: Zones 4–10.

Soil needs: Loamy, moist, well-drained soil. Fertility: rich. Amend with organic matter. Neutral 7.0 pH.

Shade degree: Partial to light shade.

Watering requirement: Water regularly; do not soak soil.

Spacing of plants: 12–18 in. (30–45 cm) apart.

Tips and care: Generally pest free. Good for beds.

IMPATIENS

One of the most popular bedding plants for the shade garden is the impatiens, known also as 'Busy Lizzie.' No retail plant stand is without six-packs of these reliable summertime growers. Because they are so ubiquitous, they are easy to bypass, but nothing beats a bank of impatiens for refreshingly bright and cheerful color in the shade garden.

Impatiens technically are perennials and carry over several years in hardiness zones 10 and 11 if not subject to frost or withering heat. In most climates, they are treated as tender annuals set out in spring, after all threat of frost has passed, and allowed to die back in autumn. They prefer fast-draining soil and plenty of watering—sometimes twice a day in hot, dry, and windy areas.

Impatiens are remarkably forgiving. Plant them 6–8 in. (15–20 cm) apart, give them ample water, and they quickly will mound up and mingle to produce a professional-looking bed or border. Impatiens tolerate light ranging from full-on sun to dense shade, although they will flower less under the latter condition.

I. wallerana is the most commonly planted impatiens species, prized for its range o bright colors and reliability in most cool-season and temperate climates. New varieties are being introduced every year, some featuring darker edges, others white eyes. For brightest color in the shade, plant a mix of all available colors. Another popular cultivar for warmer climates is New Guinea impatiens, a tropical variety with larger flowers. These impatiens require more daily sun—up to four hours—and are very hardy.

Impatiens propagate readily from cuttings, particularly if you use rooting hormone. Allow cuttings to develop in a cool, moist, indoor location, then set out rooted cuttings in spring.

Common name: Impatiens
Scientific name: *Impatiens wallerana*
Description: Slightly irregular flowers in pink, magenta, mauve, white, salmon, orange, or bicolored. Stems are succulent and erect; leaves are a glossy dark green. Plant grows in a low, mounded way 1–3 ft. (30–90 cm) tall.
Plant hardiness: Zones 3–10.
Soil needs: Moist, well-drained, sandy soil. Fertility: rich. Fertilize lightly each month with an all-purpose fertilizer. Neutral 7.0 pH.
Shade degree: Light to full shade.
Watering requirement: Water regularly.
Spacing of plants: 10–12 in. (25–30 cm) apart.
Tips and care: Works in a variety of shade situations: under shrubs or trees, by walkways, in containers. Pinch back to encourage bushiness and encourage new flower development.

Common name: Johnny-Jump-Up

Scientific name: *Viola tricolor*

Description: ¾-in.-long (18-mm) flowers are purple, white, yellow, or tricolored. Plant grows to 12 in. (30 cm) tall.

Plant hardiness: Zones 4–11.

Soil needs: Moist, well-drained soil. Fertility: moderately rich. Tolerates most soils. Neutral 7.0 pH.

Shade degree: Partial to light shade.

Watering requirement: Keep soil moist but not soggy.

Spacing of plants: 4–6 in. (10–15 cm) apart.

Tips and care: In cool, moist autumn climates, shear plants back after summer's bloom for a second, lighter flowering. Excellent for planting over bulb beds. Good in edgings, rock gardens, and containers; also as an inviting border for a vegetable bed.

Common name: Larkspur, Rocket

Scientific name: *Consolida ambigua*

Description: 1¼-in.-long (30-mm) flowers of pastel violet, rose, pink, blue, or white grow from flower spikes 1¼ in. (30 mm) long. Leaves are ferny and deeply cut. Plant grows 1–2 ft. (30–60 cm) tall, but can be grown to 5 ft. (1.5 m) tall.

Plant hardiness: Zones 4–8.

Soil needs: Moist, well-drained soil. Fertility: rich. Supplement with organic matter and feed occasionally. Alkaline 7.5 pH.

Shade degree: Partial shade.

Watering requirement: Water moderately; keep soil moist.

Spacing of plants: 8–15 in. (20–38 cm) apart, depending on anticipated height of plant.

Tips and care: Good cutting flower. Nice in massed beds and borders.

Common name: Monkey Flower, Common

Scientific name: *Mimulus guttatus*

Description: 1–2-in.-wide (25–50-mm) trumpet-shaped flowers in yellow, orange, red, or pink with succulent stems and leaves. Plant grows to about 2 ft. (60 cm) tall.

Plant hardiness: Zones 3–9.

Soil needs: Moist, well-drained soil. Fertility: moderately rich. Supplement with organic matter.

Shade degree: Partial to light shade.

Watering requirement: Water regularly; keep soil moist.

Spacing of plants: 6 in. (15 cm) apart.

Tips and care: Remove faded blossoms to promote flowering. Nice for bedding, borders, and rock gardens.

Common name: Pansy

Scientific name: *Viola* × *wittrockiana*

Description: Flat, velvety flowers in purple, maroon, blue, red, yellow, orange, or white. Leaves are heart-shaped. Plant grows to 9 in. (23 cm) tall.

Plant hardiness: Zones 3–9.

Soil needs: Moist, loamy, well-drained soil. Fertility: moderately rich. Apply liquid plant food every two weeks. Neutral 7.0 pH.

Shade degree: Partial to light shade.

Watering requirement: Deep-water regularly.

Spacing of plants: 4–6 in. (10–15 cm) apart.

Tips and care: Good in beddings and edgings. Nice cutting flower.

Common name: Primrose, English

Scientific name: *Primula polyantha*

Description: 1¹⁄₂–2-in.-wide (37–50-mm) clusters of purple, blue, rose, yellow, white, or scarlet flowers. Flat, broad-leaved rosettes of foliage grow at the base. Plant grows to 12 in. (30 cm) tall.

Plant hardiness: Zones 5–8.

Soil needs: Humus-rich, moist, well-drained soil. Fertility: rich. Supplement with peat moss or compost. Acid to neutral 6.5–7.0 pH.

Shade degree: Partial to light shade.

Watering requirement: Water regularly; do not allow soil to dry out.

Spacing of plants: 6 in. (15 cm) apart.

Tips and care: Lovely container plant. Fragrant flowers attract bees and butterflies.

Common name: Primrose, Evening

Scientific name: *Oenothera erythrosepala*

Description: 3¹⁄₂-in.-wide (8-cm) yellow poppylike flowers open at sundown. Flowers turn to red or orange over time. Plant grows 2–8 ft. (.6–2.4 m) tall.

Plant hardiness: Zones 4–9.

Soil needs: Sandy, well-drained soil. Fertility: average. Tolerates poor soils. Neutral 7.0 pH.

Shade degree: Partial shade.

Watering requirement: Water moderately.

Spacing of plants: 12–24 in. (30–60 cm) apart, depending on anticipated growth.

Tips and care: Nice as a massed planting. Good filler during summer for a border. Naturalizes in meadow landscapes.

Common name: Spider Flower
Scientific name: *Cleome hasslerana*
Description: 2–3-in.-long (5–8-cm), 6–7-in.-wide (15–18-cm) ball-shaped flowers are pink, white, or rose-purple. Bushy, sticky leaves. Plant grows 4–5 ft. (1.2–1.5 m) tall.
Plant hardiness: Zones 2–11.
Soil needs: Moist, well-drained soil. Fertility: rich. Tolerates most soils. Neutral 7.0 pH.
Shade degree: Partial to light shade.
Watering requirement: Water frequently; fairly drought tolerant.
Spacing of plants: 1½–2 ft. (45–60 cm) apart.
Tips and care: Resists pests and diseases. Nice cutting flower. Attracts hummingbirds.

Common name: Stock, Evening
Scientific name: *Matthiola longipetala*
Description: Purple to white flowers are ¾ in. (20 mm) wide and scattered throughout foliage. Leaves are gray-green and lance-shaped. Plant grows to 1½ ft. (45 cm) tall.
Plant hardiness: Zones 2–9.
Soil needs: Moist, well-drained sandy or loamy soil. Fertility: moderately rich. Neutral 7.0 pH.
Shade degree: Partial shade.
Watering requirement: Water regularly—mornings if the weather is cool, otherwise evenings.
Spacing of plants: 9–12 in. (23–30 cm) apart.
Tips and care: Good for flower beds and borders. Perfect cutting flower to scent the indoors.

Common name: Sunflower, Common
Scientific name: *Helianthus annus*
Description: 1-ft.-in-diameter (30-cm) flower heads in yellow, orange, chestnut, maroon, or bicolored with center disks of purplish-brown. Leaves are coarse, lobed, and hairy. Plant grows to 12 ft. (36 cm) tall.
Plant hardiness: Zones 4–10.
Soil needs: Dry, well-drained, loamy soil. Fertility: moderately rich. Neutral 7.0 pH.
Shade degree: Partial shade.
Watering requirement: Drought tolerant, but water well in dry periods.
Spacing of plants: 2–4 ft. (60–120 cm) apart, depending on anticipated growth.
Tips and care: Harvest flower heads for seeds as soon as they have matured.

Common name: Sweet William

Scientific name: *Dianthus barbatus*

Description: $1/3$-in.-wide (8-mm) fragrant flowers in red, rose-purple, or white are packed in dense, rounded clusters atop foliage. Bushy plant grows 3–4 ft. (90–120 cm) tall.

Plant hardiness: Zones 5–10.

Soil needs: Well-drained soil. Fertility: rich. Supplement with lime; dilute to avoid burning the tips of leaves. Neutral to alkaline 7.0–7.5 pH.

Shade degree: Partial to light shade.

Watering requirement: Water sparingly once a week; if weather is very hot, water more frequently.

Spacing of plants: 1–3 ft. (30–90 cm) apart.

Tips and care: Good for cutting beds and containers.

Common name: Tobacco, Flowering

Scientific name: *Nicotiana alata*

Description: 2–4-in.-long (5–10-cm) shiny, funnel-shaped flowers in white, pink, mauve, red, maroon, purple, or lime green. Plant grows to 5 ft. (1.5 m) tall. Compact varieties are available.

Plant hardiness: Zones 2–10.

Soil needs: Moist, well-drained soil. Fertility: moderate. Fertilize every two weeks with lime and potash. Neutral 7.0 pH.

Shade degree: Partial to light shade.

Watering requirement: Water regularly; keep soil moist in hot, dry weather.

Spacing of plants: 12–24 in. (30–60 cm) apart.

Tips and care: Good for beds, borders, and containers. Watch out for beetles.

Warning

Foliage and juice of Flowering Tobacco are hazardous if ingested. Avoid planting in areas frequented by children or pets.

Common name: Violet, Bush

Scientific name: *Browallia speciosa*

Description: 2-in.-wide (5-mm) velvety blue, violet, or white flowers. Leaves are small and green. Plant grows to 1 ft. (30 cm) tall.

Plant hardiness: Zones 10–11.

Soil needs: Moist, well-drained soil. Fertility: rich. Do not overfeed as this will lead to an overabundance of foliage at the expense of flowers. Neutral 7.0 pH.

Shade degree: Partial shade.

Watering requirement: Water by misting; keep soil moist if plant is exposed to some degree of hot sun.

Spacing of plants: 12 in. (30 cm) apart.

Tips and care: Good for containers and hanging baskets.

Common name: Wallflower

Scientific name: *Cheiranthus cheiri*

Description: Four-petaled, 1-in.-wide (25-mm) flowers in red, white, yellow, cream, lemon, apricot, salmon, pink, or purple. 3-in.-long (8-cm) narrow and pointed leaves. Plant grows 1–2½ ft. (30–75 cm) tall.

Plant hardiness: Zones 6–9.

Soil needs: Moist, well-drained, loamy soil. Fertility: rich. Tolerates poor soils. Neutral to alkaline 7.0–7.5 pH.

Shade degree: Partial shade.

Watering requirement: Water regularly.

Spacing of plants: 6–12 in. (15–30 cm) apart.

Tips and care: Flowers are aromatic. Nice cutting flower and companion for spring bulbs. Works well in containers.

On this June day the buds in my garden are almost as enchanting as the open flowers. Things in bud bring, in the heat of a June noontide, the recollection of the loveliest days of the year—those days in May when all is suggested, nothing yet fulfilled.

MRS. FRANCIS KING

Common name: Wishbone Flower

Scientific name: *Torenia fournieri*

Description: 1-in.-wide (25-mm) flowers in purple-blue, white with purplish spots, pink, or white, with a yellow throat. Leaves are oval. Plant grows 10–12 in. (25–30 cm) tall.

Plant hardiness: Zones 4–11.

Soil needs: Very moist, well-drained soil. Fertility: rich. Supplement with peat moss or organic matter, especially if soil has a high clay content. Neutral 7.0 pH.

Shade degree: Partial to light shade.

Watering requirement: Water regularly and well.

Spacing of plants: 6–8 in. (15–20 cm) apart.

Tips and care: Nice in borders, edgings, and containers.

PERENNIALS

Common name: Anemone, Japanese
Scientific name: *Anemone × hybrida*
Description: 2–3 in. (5–8 cm) pink or white flowers rise above a foot-high (30-cm) mound of foliage on stalks that reach up to 5 ft. (1.5 m) tall. Leaves are dark green and deeply lobed. In winter, cottonball-like seed heads cover the stems.
Plant hardiness: Zones 6–10.
Soil needs: Well-drained soil. Fertility: rich. Supplement with peat moss. Neutral 7.0 pH.
Shade degree: Partial to light shade.
Watering requirement: Water moderately.
Spacing of plants: 18 in. (45 cm) apart.
Tips and care: Can be intrusive. Nice for large borders and rock gardens. Protect from wind.

Green is the fresh emblem of well-founded hopes. In blue the spirit can wander, but in green it can rest.

MARY WEBB

Common name: Bellflower, Great
Scientific name: *Campanula latifolia*
Description: 1½-in.-long (37-mm) purplish-blue bell-shaped flowers. Dark-green leaves are 3 in. (8 cm) long and have a broad, lancelike shape. Plant grows 2–4 ft. (.6–1.2 cm) tall.
Plant hardiness: Zones 4–7.
Soil needs: Moist, well-drained sandy or gravelly soil. Fertility: rich. Neutral to alkaline 7.0–7.5 pH.
Shade degree: Partial to light shade.
Watering requirement: Water regularly, especially in hot, dry weather.
Spacing of plants: 12–18 in. (30–45 cm) apart.
Tips and care: Cut flowers as they fade to keep plant vigorous. Works well for the back of a border. Nice cutting flower. Watch out for slugs.

Common name: Bergenia
Scientific name: *Bergenia*
Description: 3–6-in.-wide (8–15-cm) flower clusters with pink, white, or purplish-pink blooms. Glossy, cabbagelike leaves stay green year-round in warmer climates. Plant grows in a dense clump that reaches 18 in. (45 cm) tall.
Plant hardiness: Zones 4–10.
Soil needs: Moist soil. Fertility: poor, which actually boosts leaf color. Neutral 7.0 pH.
Shade degree: Light to full shade.
Watering requirement: Water moderately, less if in dense shade.
Spacing of plants: 12–15 in. (30–38 cm) apart.
Tips and care: Nice for borders, edgings, and as a ground cover. Watch out for slugs.

Common name: Bleeding Heart
Scientific name: *Dicentra spectabilis*
Description: 1-in. (25-mm) deep-pink, heart-shaped flowers with white inner petals "bleed" down from arched stems. Foliage is ferny, graceful, and a light blue-green. Plant grows 1–3 ft. (30–90 cm) tall.
Plant hardiness: Zones 4–10.
Soil needs: Moist, well-drained soil. Fertility: rich. Supplement with peat moss or leaf mold. Neutral 7.0 pH.
Shade degree: Partial to full shade.
Watering requirement: Water regularly.
Spacing of plants: 2–2½ ft. (60–75 cm) apart.
Tips and care: Good for rock gardens and borders. If hot, dry weather causes foliage to droop and flag, cut plant to the ground.

Common name: Bluebells, Virginia
Scientific name: *Mertensia virginica*
Description: Dainty, 1-in. (25-mm) nodding bells of purplish or pale blue rest atop slender stems 1–2 ft. (30–60 cm) tall. Apple-green leaves are narrow and form leafy clumps 2 ft. (60 cm) tall.
Plant hardiness: Zones 4–8.
Soil needs: Moist, well-drained soil. Fertility: rich. Acid 7.5 pH.
Shade degree: Partial to full shade.
Watering requirement: Water regularly during bloom period; allow soil to dry out when plant is dormant in summer.
Spacing of plants: 1½ ft. (45 cm) apart.
Tips and care: Likes moist spots. Attracts bees. Makes a nice companion to tulips and daffodils.

Common name: Bluestar
Scientific name: *Amsonia tabernaemontana*
Description: Starlike flowers bloom in dense, pale-blue clusters atop long stems. Leaves are willowy; fall foliage is yellow. Plant grows to 2 ft. (60 cm) tall.
Plant hardiness: Zones 4–10.
Soil needs: Moist, average soil. Fertility: moderately rich. Neutral 7.0 pH.
Shade degree: Partial to light shade.
Watering requirement: Water regularly.
Spacing of plants: 6–9 in. (15–23 cm) apart.
Tips and care: Nice cutting and border flower. Prune yearly for form and growth.

Common name: Calceolaria
Scientific name: *Calceolaria*
Description: Pouchlike flowers of yellow, red, pink, maroon, or bronze with green or purple markings grow in irregular clusters. Plant grows to 6 in. (15 cm) tall.
Plant hardiness: Zones 7–11.
Soil needs: Moist, well-drained soil. Fertility: moderately rich. Neutral 7.0 pH.
Shade degree: Partial to light shade.
Watering requirement: Water moderately; let soil dry out between waterings.
Spacing of plants: 6–9 in. (15–23 cm) apart.
Tips and care: Known also as slipper flower or pocketbook flower, depending on the cultivar. Good for beds and borders and in woodland settings. Watch out for spider mites.

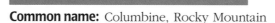

Common name: Columbine, Rocky Mountain
Scientific name: *Aquilegia caerula*
Description: Airy 2–3-in.-wide (5–8-cm) pastel blue and white flowers rise atop clumps of deeply lobed green leaves. Plant grows 2–3 ft. (60-90 cm) tall.
Plant hardiness: Zones 3–10.
Soil needs: Moist, well-drained soil. Fertility: rich. Supplement with organic matter. Neutral 7.0 pH.
Shade degree: Partial to light shade.
Watering requirement: Water regularly, does not tolerate dry soils.
Spacing of plants: 10–15 in. (25–38 cm) apart.
Tips and care: Attracts hummingbirds to its delicate flowers. Excellent cutting flower.

Common name: Coralbells

Scientific name: *Heuchera sanguinea*

Description: Bell-shaped red flowers dangle from slender stems above mounded, heart-shaped evergreen leaves and bell-shaped flowers. Plant grows 1–2 ft. (30–6 cm) tall.

Plant hardiness: Zones 4–9.

Soil needs: Moist, well-drained soil. Fertility: rich. Supplement with organic matter. Acid to neutral 6.0–7.0 pH.

Shade degree: Partial shade.

Watering requirement: Water moderately.

Spacing of plants: 10–15 in. (25–38 cm) apart.

Tips and care: Native of the Southwest. Works well in rock gardens, borders, raised beds, or on retaining walls. Nice cutting flower. In hot-summer areas, sow in locations with partial shade.

Common name: Coreopsis, Threadleaf

Scientific name: *Coreopsis verticillata*

Description: 2-in.-in-diameter (50-mm) yellow, star-shaped, daisylike flowers. Leaves are narrow, finely divided, and threadlike. Plant grows in an upright clumping manner 2–3 ft. (60-90 cm) tall. Dwarf varieties are available 6–10 in. (15–25 cm) tall.

Plant hardiness: Zones 4–10.

Soil needs: Well-drained soil. Fertility: average. Tolerates poor soils. Acid to alkaline 6.5–7.5 pH.

Watering requirement: Drought tolerant, but carefully monitor in very hot and dry conditions.

Spacing of plants: 12 in. (30 cm) apart.

Tips and care: Excellent cutting flower. Works well in a mass planting or meadow garden.

Common name: Foxglove, Yellow

Scientific name: *Digitalis grandiflora*

Description: 1–3-in.-long (25–75-mm) creamy yellow flowers speckled with brown line spirelike stalks. Leaves are coarse and fuzzy. Plant grows 2–3 ft. (60–90 cm) tall.

Plant hardiness: Zones 4–9.

Soil needs: Moist, well-drained soil. Fertility: rich. Supplement with leaf mold. Acid to neutral 6.5–7.0 pH.

Shade degree: Partial to light shade, full shade if climate is very hot.

Watering requirement: Water regularly.

Spacing of plants: 15–18 in. (38–45 cm) apart.

Tips and care: Nice for borders. Good cutting flower. Digitalis, the heart stimulant, comes from the leaves. Poorly suited to humid, coastal climates.

Common name: Geranium, Wild
Scientific name: *Geranium maculatum*
Description: Spotted five-petaled pale lilac or violet flowers bloom in loose clusters. 3–6-in.-wide (8–15-cm) leaves are deeply cut in 3–5 divisions. Plant grows 1–2 ft. (30–60 cm) tall.
Plant hardiness: Zones 5–8.
Soil needs: Moist, well-drained, loamy soil. Fertility: rich. Acid to neutral 6.0–7.0 pH.
Shade degree: Partial to light shade.
Watering requirement: Water regularly.
Spacing of plants: 10–15 in. (25–38 cm) apart.
Tips and care: Good in borders or wildflower gardens. Extracts from this plant are used for intestinal disorders.

Common name: Iris, Crested
Scientific name: *Iris cristata*
Description: Delicate lilac-blue flowers with yellow crests. Narrow-bladed, light-green leaves die back in autumn. Plant grows 4–6 in. (10–15 cm) tall.
Plant hardiness: Zones 4–9.
Soil needs: Moist, well-drained, humus-rich soil. Fertility: moderately rich. Acid 6.5 pH.
Shade degree: Open to partial shade.
Watering requirement: Water regularly.
Spacing of plants: 6–12 in. (15–30 cm) apart.
Tips and care: A wildflower of southeastern woodlands also works well as a ground cover for river banks and steep slopes. Shallow but numerous roots.

Common name: Jack-in-the-Pulpit
Scientific name: *Arisaema triphyllum*
Description: 3-in.-long (75-mm) green, fingerlike flowers sheathed in arched "pulpits" made of leaflike spathe. Leaves are 4–6 in. (10–15 cm) long and grouped in threes. In autumn, plant bears cone-shaped clusters of bright-red, inedible berries.
Plant hardiness: Zones 5–8.
Soil needs: Moist, humus rich soil. Fertility: rich. Acid 6.5 pH.
Shade degree: Open to deep shade.
Watering requirement: Water regularly; dry soil may stunt growth.
Tips and care: Works nicely in a naturalized setting, especially with ferns. In the wild, it grows along rivers and near waterfalls.

Warning

Roots of Jack-in-the-Pulpit are very poisonous, though Native Americans used this plant as a natural medicine. Avoid planting in areas frequented by children or pets.

Common name: Lily, Toad

Scientific name: *Tricyrtis hirta*

Description: 1-in.-long (25-mm) bell-shaped whitish flowers heavily spotted with black and purple markings inside bloom between broad, symmetrical leaves arranged in formal pairs. Plant grows to 3 ft. (90 cm) tall.

Plant hardiness: Zones 6–10.

Soil needs: Moist, well-drained soil. Fertility: rich. Supplement with peat moss, compost, or leaf mold. Neutral 7.0 pH.

Shade degree: Partial to full shade.

Watering requirement: Water regularly.

Spacing of plants: 12–18 in. (30–45 cm) apart.

Tips and care: Works well for wildflower "nooks" and rock gardens. Nice planted with ferns. Prune off dead foliage in late autumn or early winter. Flowers are often described as resembling orchids.

Common name: Lupine

Scientific name: *Lupinus*

Warning

All parts of the Lupine plant are hazardous if ingested. Avoid planting in areas frequented by children or pets.

Description: ½–1-in.-wide (13–25-mm) sweet pea–like flowers in orange, yellow, white, blue, and purple along 1–3-ft.-tall (30–90-cm) spires. Leaves are a soft blue-green and divided. Plant grows 2–3 ft. (60–90 cm) tall.

Plant hardiness: Zones 5–8.

Soil needs: Well-drained, moist soil. Fertility: rich. Acid to alkaline 6.5–7.5 pH.

Shade degree: Partial shade.

Watering requirement: Water regularly.

Spacing of plants: 8–10 in. (20–25 cm) apart.

Tips and care: Works well in borders. Good cutting flower. Nick seeds before planting. Watch out for aphids.

Common name: Mallow, Hollyhock

Scientific name: *Malva alcea*

Description: Delicate, 2-in.-wide (50-mm) flowers in pink or white rise on loose spikes amid bushy clumps of foliage. Leaves are fuzzy and divided. Plant grows 2–4 ft. (60–120 cm) tall.

Plant hardiness: Zones 4–10.

Soil needs: Dry, well-drained soil. Tolerates poor soils. In hot climates, add organic matter to help roots reach for moisture. Neutral to alkaline 7.0–7.5 pH.

Shade degree: Light to partial shade.

Watering requirement: Water conservatively.

Spacing of plants: 12 in. (30 cm) apart.

Tips and care: Works well in borders. Low maintenance.

Common name: Meadow Sweet
Scientific name: *Astilbe tacquetii*
Description: Pink or reddish-purple flowers cluster densely on long spikes. Fernlike bronze-green leaves. Plant grows 3–4 ft. (90–120 cm) tall and 2–3 ft. (60–90 cm) wide.
Plant hardiness: Zones 4–9.
Soil needs: Moist, well-drained soil. Fertility: rich. Supplement with peat moss or compost; fertilize monthly during the growing season. Neutral 7.0 pH.
Shade degree: Partial shade.
Watering requirement: Water frequently for sandy soil, otherwise moderately.
Spacing of plants: 15–18 in. (38–45 cm) apart.
Tips and care: Nice in mixed borders and beds. Pest free. Drought tolerant.

Common name: Monkshood, Common
Scientific name: *Aconitum napellus*
Description: 1–2-in.-long (25–50-mm) purple-blue helmetlike flowers rise from tall spikes. Leaves are dark green with deep-toothed cuts. Plant grows 3–4 ft. (90–120 cm) tall.
Plant hardiness: Zones 5–9.
Soil needs: Moist, well-drained soil. Fertility: rich. Supplement with compost or leaf mold. Acid to neutral 6.5–7.0 pH.
Shade degree: Partial shade.
Watering requirement: Water regularly.
Spacing of plants: 12–18 in. (30–45 cm) apart.
Tips and care: Good for woodlands. Nice cutting flower. The drug aconite, which is used to relieve pain, is derived from the plant.

Warning

Roots, leaves, and seeds of Common Monkshood are toxic if ingested. Store seeds in childproof containers, and avoid planting in areas frequented by children or pets.

Common name: Navelwort
Scientific name: *Omphalodes cappadocica*
Description: Bright-blue flowers with starlike centers grow from green foliage. Plant grows 6–10 in. (15–25 cm) tall.
Plant hardiness: Zones 6–10.
Soil needs: Moist, well-drained soil. Fertility: average to rich. Alkaline 7.5 pH.
Shade degree: Partial to full shade.
Watering requirement: Water moderately; tolerates dryness.
Spacing of plants: 10 in. (25 cm) apart.
Tips and care: Works best in woodsy settings. Plant with bulbs and wildflowers.

Common name: Peach-Bells

Scientific name: *Campanula persicifolia*

Description: 2-in.-long (5-mm) blue, white, or lavender cupped-shaped flowers bloom on 2–3-ft.-tall (60–90-cm) stems. Peach- and bright-green-colored, lance-shaped, narrow leaves are 4–8 in. (10–20 cm) long. Plant grows to 3 ft. (90 cm) tall and about 1 ft. (30 cm) wide.

Plant hardiness: Zones 3–8.

Soil needs: Moist, well-drained soil. Fertility: moderately rich. Neutral 7.0 pH.

Shade degree: Partial to light shade.

Watering requirement: Water regularly.

Spacing of plants: 12–18 in. (30–45 cm) apart.

Tips and care: Works well for the middle or back of a border and in mixed beds. Cut flowers as they fade to ensure plant vigor. Watch out for slugs.

Common name: Poppy, Welsh

Scientific name: *Meconopsis cambrica*

Description: 2-in.-wide (50-mm), four-petaled yellow or orange flowers bloom along slender stems. Feathery leaves form large tufts about 1 ft. (30 cm) wide. Plant grows to 2 ft. (60 cm) tall.

Plant hardiness: Zones 6–8.

Soil needs: Moist, humus-rich, well-drained soil. Fertility: rich. Amend with peat moss or manure. Acid to neutral 6.5–7.0 pH.

Shade degree: Partial to light shade.

Watering requirement: Water regularly; do not allow soil to dry out.

Spacing of plants: 12–18 in. (30–45 cm) apart.

Tips and care: Good for shady woodland settings or rock gardens.

Common name: Primrose, English

Scientific name: *Primula vulgaris*

Description: Flowers in red, purple, yellow, white, or blue with a yellow eye resemble miniature roses and grow from slender, hairy, leafless stalks. Leaves are broad, lance-shaped, and wrinkled. Plant grows to 6 in. (15 cm) tall.

Plant hardiness: Zones 5–8.

Soil needs: Moist, well-drained soil. Fertility: moderately rich. Slightly acid to neutral 6.5–7.0 pH.

Shade degree: Light shade.

Watering requirement: Water regularly.

Spacing of plants: 6–12 in. (15–30 cm) apart.

Tips and care: Nice for English borders and as a low component of other flower beds. Fragrant flowers. Watch out for slugs and root weevils.

Common name: Queen-of-the-Prairie

Scientific name: *Filipendula rubra*

Description: Foot-long (30-cm) clusters of tiny magenta flowers. Leaves are feathery. Plant grows in a lush clump to 7 ft. (2 m) tall and about 3 ft. (90 cm) wide.

Plant hardiness: Zones 3–8.

Soil needs: Moist, well-drained soil. Fertility: moderately rich. Alkaline 7.5 pH.

Shade degree: Light to partial shade.

Watering requirement: Water regularly; keep soil moist.

Spacing of plants: 2–3 ft. (60–90 cm) apart.

Tips and care: Impressive cutting flower. Nice in summer borders or at the rear of a bed.

Common name: Rose, Lenten

Scientific name: *Helleborous orientalis*

Description: Cream or purple-pink flowers. Shiny, dark, leathery leaves. Plant grows 12–18 in. (30–45 cm) tall.

Plant hardiness: Zones 5–9.

Soil needs: Well-drained, moist soil. Fertility: rich. Supplement with peat moss, leaf mold, or compost. Neutral to alkaline 7.0–7.5 pH.

Shade degree: Open to full shade.

Watering requirement: Water regularly.

Spacing of plants: 12–15 in. (30–38 cm) apart.

Tips and care: Pest free. Nice in a rock garden or by a door, pathway, or stairway.

Warning

Roots of Lenten Rose are toxic if ingested. Avoid planting in areas frequented by children or pets.

Common name: Sweet William, Wild

Scientific name: *Phlox divaricata*

Description: Less-than-1-in.-wide (25-mm) purple-blue flowers cluster loosely atop upright stems. Leaves are narrow. Plant grows 8–18 in. (20–45 cm) tall and spreads rapidly by means of creeping stems.

Plant hardiness: Zones 4–9.

Soil needs: Moist, well-drained, humus-rich soil. Fertility: moderately rich. Acid to neutral 6.5–7.0 pH.

Shade degree: Partial to full shade.

Watering requirement: Water moderately.

Spacing of plants: 8–12 in. (20–30 cm) apart.

Tips and care: A native of open woods and meadows from Quebec to Florida and west to Nebraska. Nice for woodlands or wildflower borders. Attracts butterflies.

Common name: Trillium, Snow
Scientific name: *Trillium grandiflorum*
Description: 2–3-in.-wide (5–8-cm) white flowers that fading
to pink with time. Leaves are oval, deep green, and up to 6 in.
(15 cm) long. Plant grows 12–18 in. (30–45 cm) tall.
Plant hardiness: Zones 5–9.
Soil needs: Constantly moist, well-drained, humus soil.
Fertility: rich. Acid to neutral 6.5–7.0 pH.
Shade degree: Partial to full shade.
Watering requirement: Water well and often.
Spacing of plants: 5–8 in. (13–20 cm) apart.
Tips and care: Works well as a ground cover. Good for
wildflower gardens and nooks, in woodland settings, and in mass plantings near
rocks and ferns. Don't cut back leaves after the season, they will provide
nourishment for the following year.

*Scents bring memories, and many memories bring
nostalgic pleasure. We would be wise to plan for
this when we plant a garden.*

THALASSA CRUSO

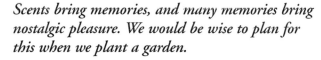

Common name: Violet, Sweet
Scientific name: *Viola odorata*
Description: Fragrant ¾-in.-wide (18-mm) purple, pink, or
white blooms. Leaves are heart-shaped, crinkly, and form
clumps. Plant grows 6–8 in. (15–20 cm) tall and about 3 in.
(8 cm) wide.
Plant hardiness: Zones 6–10.
Soil needs: Moist, well-drained soil. Fertility: rich. Supplement
with compost, leaf mold, or manure. Acid to slightly alkaline
6.5–7.5 pH.
Shade degree: Partial shade.
Watering requirement: Water moderately; regularly during dry periods.
Spacing of plants: 10–12 in. (25–30 cm) apart.
Tips and care: Flower is candied and used as a confection or decoration for cakes.
High in vitamins A and C. Works well as a ground cover. Good for a children's
garden. Watch out for red spider mites.

SHRUBS

Common name: Aucuba, Japanese
Scientific name: *Aucuba japonica*
Description: Bushy and dense evergreen plant with ½-in. (13-mm) scarlet berries reaches 3 ft. (90 cm) tall. Oval leaves are glossy and 4–6 in. (10–15 cm) long; certain cultivars have gold dots or markings. Small purple flowers bloom in spring.
Plant hardiness: Zones 8–10.
Soil needs: Dry to moist, well-drained soil. Fertility: rich. Fertilize new plants after 6 months; established plants every 3–4 months. Acid 6.5 pH.
Shade degree: Dappled, partial shade.
Watering requirement: Keep soil slightly moist; drought tolerant.
Spacing of plants: 3 ft. (90 cm) apart.
Tips and care: Very popular in southern U.S. Cut back in winter or early spring before new growth starts. Watch out for spider mites.

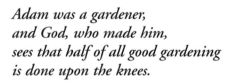

Adam was a gardener,
and God, who made him,
sees that half of all good gardening
is done upon the knees.

RUDYARD KIPLING

Common name: Azalea, Kurume
Scientific name: *Rhododendron*
Description: Evergreen plant with ½–1½-in. (13–38-cm) flowers in pink, purple, red, or white reaches 4–6 ft. (1.2–1.8 m) tall.
Plant hardiness: Zones 7–9.
Soil needs: Moist, well-drained, peat-rich soil. Fertility: rich. Add organic matter before planting. Acid 6.5 pH.
Shade degree: Partial to light shade.
Watering requirement: Water regularly.
Spacing of plants: 4–6 ft. (1.2–1.8 m) apart.
Tips and care: Prune lightly. Nice accent plant against evergreen trees. Susceptible to root and crown rot.

Common name: Buckeye, Bottle-brush

Scientific name: *Aesculus parviflora*

Description: Dense, layered mounds of deep-green foliage topped by foot-long (30-cm) spikes with ½-in. (13-mm) white flowers that have long, pink-tipped stamens. Leaves are palm-shaped and turn yellow in autumn. Plant grows 3–10 ft. (.9–3 m) tall and wide.

Plant hardiness: Zones 4–10.

Soil needs: Average, moist, well-drained soil. Fertility: moderate. Enrich with peat moss or leaf mold. Neutral 7.0 pH.

Shade degree: Light shade.

Watering requirement: Water moderately.

Spacing of plants: 10 ft. (3 m) apart.

Tips and care: Native to the southeastern U.S. Makes a nice rustic thicket or accent plant against evergreen trees. Pruning is not required.

Common name: Butterfly Bush

Scientific name: *Buddleia alternifolia*

Description: Fountain-shaped, woody shrub with lilac-purple, bell-shaped fragrant flowers grows 10–20 ft. (3–6 m) tall. Leaves are willowlike, 1–4 in. (25–100 mm) long and light green with a silvery underside. Branches are long and delicately bent.

Plant hardiness: Zones 5–10.

Soil needs: Well-drained soil. Fertility: moderately rich. Supplement with peat moss, leaf mold, or compost. Neutral 7.0 pH.

Shade degree: Partial shade, especially in the afternoon.

Watering requirement: Water moderately; somewhat drought tolerant.

Spacing of plants: 5–10 ft. (1.5–3 m) apart.

Tips and care: Attracts butterflies, hummingbirds, and bees. Excellent as an ornamental hedge and for borders. Nice cutting flower .

Common name: Camellia, Common

Scientific name: *Camellia japonica*

Description: Slow-growing evergreen shrub with 2–9-in.-wide (5–23-cm) red, white, pink, or multicolored flowers with multiple petals grows 6–10 ft. (1.8–3 m) tall and can reach 30 ft. (9 m) tall. Shiny, waxy, dark-green leaves are 2½–4 in. (6–10 cm) long.

Plant hardiness: Zones 8–10.

Soil needs: Moist, well-drained soil. Fertility: rich. Fertilize every 2 months. Acid 7.5 pH.

Shade degree: Open shade.

Watering requirement: Keep soil evenly moist.

Spacing of plants: 3–5 ft. (.9–1.5 m) apart.

Tips and care: Makes a beautiful hedge or screen for walls. Nice accent plant.

Common name: Camellia, Sasanqua
Scientific name: *Camellia sasanqua*
Description: Deciduous shrub with rose, white, or red flowers grows 5–6 ft. (1.5–1.8 m) tall and can reach 20 ft. (6 m) tall. Leaves are slender, shiny, dark green and 2 in. (5 cm) long.
Plant hardiness: Zones 8–10.
Soil needs: Moist, well-drained soil. Fertility: rich. Acid to neutral 6.5–7.0 pH.
Shade degree: Partial to light shade.
Watering requirement: Keep soil evenly moist.
Spacing of plants: 2–3 ft. (60–90 cm) apart.
Tips and care: Shelter from winter winds and heavy rains. Nice informal hedge.

Common name: Cotoneaster, Spreading
Scientific name: *Cotoneaster divaricatus*
Description: Deciduous shrub with 1/2-in. (13-mm) pink flowers, dark-green leaves, and 1/2-in. (13-mm) red berries grows 5–6 ft. (1.5–1.8 m) tall and 8–10 ft. (2.4–3 m) wide.
Plant hardiness: Zones 5–10.
Soil needs: Moist, well-drained soil. Fertility: low to moderate. Acid to neutral 6.5–7.0 pH.
Shade degree: Partial shade.
Watering requirement: Water moderately.
Spacing of plants: 5 ft. (1.5 m) apart.
Tips and care: Attracts chipmunks and birds. Requires minimal pruning.

Common name: Gardenia, Common
Scientific name: *Gardenia jasminoides*
Description: Elegant evergreen shrub with very aromatic 2–3 1/2-in.-wide (5–9-cm) flowers grows 4–6 ft. (1.2–1.8 m) tall. Leaves are thick, glossy, dark green, and 3–4 in. (8–10 cm) long.
Plant hardiness: Zones 8–11.
Soil needs: Moist, well-drained, rich soil. Fertility: moderate. Supplement with peat or organic matter. Very acid 4.5–5.5 pH.
Shade degree: Partial to light shade.
Watering requirement: Water regularly; keep soil evenly moist.
Spacing of plants: 2–3 ft. (60–90 cm) apart.
Tips and care: Deadhead to encourage new flowers. Prune to shape after final bloom. Works well as an informal hedge, as a container plant, or along streams or by rocks. Watch out for aphids, scale, mealybugs, and spider mites.

HYDRANGEA

For sheer lushness and a truly elegant look, hydrangeas are the perfect shade shrub. Some grow to immense sizes—a 6-foot (1.8-m) height and 8-foot (2.4-m) spread is not uncommon, and some reach 12 feet (4 m) high—while others contain themselves to 2-to-4-foot (50–120-cm) spreads and can be pruned to stay compact. Hydrangeas range in color from white to various clear shades of pink and mauve, and from light to deep blue and purple-blue. Best of all, their deep-green, textured leaves are as lush as their heavy flower heads.

Hydrangeas prefer shade, though some need a few hours of direct light each day to flower abundantly. Two species—*H. serrata* and *H. sargentiana*—flourish in shade. All hydrangeas need plenty of moisture and rich, loose soil.

H. macrophylla, the garden hydrangea, is perhaps the best known. It comes essentially in two forms—the delicate lace cap, which has plate-sized white or bluish-pink clusters of sterile flowers surrounding fertile florets; and the ball-shaped mophead, which comes in clear shades of pink and red-pink. The ever-accommodating hydrangea shifts its color depending on the pH of the soil: acid soil will bring on the blue color and alkaline the pink. About a pound (0.5 kg) of aluminum sulfate applied to a good-sized bush in autumn will give you blue flowers the following summer, especially if you keep dosing the plant with a weak solution of epsom salts (about an ounce [28 g] per gallon [3.8 l] of water) every few weeks in the spring. Likewise, an amendment of lime to the soil will ensure pink flowers.

Some consider the mophead a solid choice for a formal shade garden, and a bank of them in bloom is a truly beautiful sight. Lace caps, with their rangy growth, suit a woodland or less formal shade garden. Another beauty is *H. quercifolia,* or oakleaf hydrangea, with its large, lobed "oak" leaves that produce short, white-flowered spires in early summer. *H. anomala* is a good choice of hydrangea for clambering up a wall or over an arbor.

Common name: Hydrangea

Scientific name: *Hydrangea macrophylla*

Description: Deciduous shrub with handsome, round flower heads in pink, blue, purple, or red. Leaves are broad, oval, and dark green.

Plant hardiness: Zones 6–10.

Soil needs: Moist, well-drained, loamy soil. Supplement with compost, peat moss, or leaf mold. Acid to alkaline 6.5–7.5 pH. Blue and purple flowers bloom in acidic soil—add aluminum sulfate; reds and pinks in neutral to alkaline soil—add lime.

Shade degree: Partial shade.

Watering requirement: Keep soil moist.

Spacing of plants: 6–10 ft. (1.8–3 m) apart.

Tips and care: Cut and dry flower heads for wreaths and floral arrangements.

Common name: Japanese Maple, Cutleaf
Scientific name: *Acer palmatum* 'Dissectum'
Description: Slow-growing dwarf grows to 12 ft. (3.6 m) tall and wide. Leaves are indented, finely cut, 3–4 in. (8–10 cm) long, and turn brilliant red in autumn. At maturity, it forms a dense, broad mound of weeping branches.
Plant hardiness: Zones 5–9.
Soil needs: Moist, well-drained soil. Fertility: moderately rich. Supplement with leaf mold or peat moss. Acid 6.5 pH.
Shade degree: Open to partial shade.
Watering requirement: Water moderately.
Spacing of plants: 12 ft. (3.6 m) apart.
Tips and care: Good for average-sized yards, entryways, and patios. Prune for small spaces. Fairly disease resistant.

Common name: Mock Orange
Scientific name: *Philadelphus coronarius*
Description: Rapidly growing shrub with intensely fragrant 1-in. (25-mm) creamy white flowers grows 10 ft. (3 m) tall and wide. Leaves are dull green, 1–3 in. (25–75 mm) long, pointed, and oval.
Plant hardiness: Zones 4–9.
Soil needs: Moist, well-drained soil. Fertility: moderately rich. Supplement with peat moss, leaf mold, or compost. Neutral 7.5 pH.
Shade degree: Partial to light shade.
Watering requirement: Water regularly.
Spacing of plants: 5 ft. (1.5 m) apart.
Tips and care: Good for hedges. Pest and disease resistant.

Common name: Rhododendron, Korean
Scientific name: *Rhododendron mucronulation*
Description: Deciduous shrub with 1½-in.-wide (38-cm) bell-shaped flowers in rosy purple. Leaves are narrow, 1–3 in. (25–75 mm) long, deep green, and turn a yellow-bronze in autumn.
Plant hardiness: Zones 5–9.
Soil needs: Moist, well-drained, peat-rich soil. Fertility: rich. Add organic matter before planting. Acid 6.5 pH.
Shade degree: Partial to light shade.
Watering requirement: Water regularly.
Spacing of plants: Best planted alone.
Tips and care: Mulch with pine needles or compost to protect plant from frost.

Common name: Viburnum

Scientific name: *Viburnum dilatatum*

Description: Deciduous shrub with clusters of 5-in.-wide (13-cm) white flowers followed by scarlet berries in autumn grows 6–10 ft. (1.8–3 m) tall. Leaves are rounded, 4–5 in. (10–13 cm) long, hairy, coarsely toothed, and turn orange-red in autumn.

Plant hardiness: Zones 5–8.

Soil needs: Moist, well-drained soil. Fertility: rich. Slightly acid to neutral 6.5–7.0 pH.

Shade degree: Partial to light shade.

Watering requirement: Water regularly.

Spacing of plants: 6–10 ft. (1.8–3 m) apart.

Tips and care: Attracts birds. Works well in mixed borders.

Morning is the best of all times in the garden. The sun is not yet hot. Sweet vapors rise from the earth. Night dew clings to the soil and makes plants glisten. Birds call to one another. Bees are already at work.

WILLIAM LONGGOOD

Common name: Witch Hazel, Common

Scientific name: *Hamamelis virginiana*

Description: Rounded shrub with fragrant, ribbonlike, bright-yellow flowers grows to 20 ft. (6 m) tall and wide. Flowers bloom on bare twigs after foliage yellows and drops. Leaves are 4–6 in. (10–15 cm) long, oval, and coarse.

Plant hardiness: Zones 5–9.

Soil needs: Light, moist, well-drained soil. Fertility: rich. Acid 6.5 pH.

Shade degree: Partial shade.

Watering requirement: Water moderately.

Spacing of plants: 20 ft. (6 m) apart.

Tips and care: "Urban stress" specimen tolerant of dry, polluted air. Rarely needs pruning. Named after forked twigs used as divining rods for water witching, and, distilled, for witch-hazel lotion, used to treat sprains, eczema, and varicose veins.

GROUND COVERS

Common name: Bunchberry
Scientific name: *Cornus canadensis*
Description: Ornamental deciduous ground cover with pincushions of tiny white flowers followed by shiny red berries grows to 6 in. (15 cm) tall. Leaves are 2 in. (50 mm) long, dark green, and turn red in autumn.
Plant hardiness: Zones 2–7.
Soil needs: Moist, well-drained, soil. Fertility: rich. Supplement with peat moss. Acid 6.5 pH.
Shade degree: Partial to full shade.
Watering requirement: Water frequently until plants are established; then keep soil moist but not soggy.
Spacing of plants: 6 in. (15 cm) apart.
Tips and care: Member of the dogwood family. Well suited to woodland settings. Works well in mixed borders and wildlife thickets.

HOSTAS

Among shade plants renowned for their foliage, hostas reign supreme. One reason is their great diversity of size, color, and texture. Some create mounds 6 inches (15 cm) high; others grow to 4 feet (120 cm) wide with 6-foot (1.8-m) flower spires. They may be solid blue-green, green and chartreuse, or variegated with cream or white. Leaves can be smooth, dimpled, or wrinkled.

Hostas are very adaptable and thrive in full to light shade. Plant them in humus-rich soil, give them adequate watering, and they will perform like troupers, hardly needing division for years to come.

Some of the acknowledged favorites include giants like *H.* 'Blue Umbrellas,' with its large blue-green leaves that have bold ribbing; *H. sieboldiana* 'Elegans,' a deep blue-gray plant that grows to form 4-foot (1-m) mounds; and *H. venusta*, a dark-green dwarf that mounds to 6 inches (15 cm) high. *H. fortunei* 'Aureo Marginata' features large, deep-green leaves with gold edging that turns to cream, and *H.* 'Gold Standard' changes from light green with deep-green margins to gold with light-green margins. Both grow 1–2 feet (31–60 cm) high, making them perfect front- and midborder plants.

Hostas make fine counterpoints to ferns and mosses, and midsize varieties mound beautifully on path edges. They also make perfect shade plants, with one hitch: snails, slugs, and earwigs love them. Avoid pesticides by burying saucers filled with beer (yes, beer) at soil level. Snails and slugs will crawl in and not care if they ever leave.

Common name: Hosta, Narrowleaf; or Plaintain Lily
Scientific name: *Hosta lancifolia*
Description: Fast-growing ground cover with 2-in. (50-mm) violet flowers supported by strong, upright stalks grows 2 ft. (60 cm) tall. Leaves are 4–6 in. (10–15 cm) long, narrow, deep green, glossy, and form cascading mounds.
Plant hardiness: Zones 4–9.
Soil needs: Moist, well-drained, humus rich-soil. Fertility: rich. Neutral 7.0 pH.
Shade degree: Light to full shade.
Watering requirement: Water regularly.
Spacing of plants: 18 in. (45 cm) apart.
Tips and care: Native of Japan, China, and Korea. Excellent for mass plantings. Watch out for snails and slugs.

Common name: Phlox, Creeping
Scientific name: *Phlox stolonifera*
Description: Low-growing ground cover with 1-in.-wide (25-mm) soft blue or purple loose clusters of flowers grows 6–12 in. (15–30 cm) tall and 2 ft. (60 cm) wide. Leaves are broad, oval, covered with downy hair, and about 1½ in. (38 mm) wide.
Plant hardiness: Zones 4–8.
Soil needs: Moist, well-drained soil. Fertility: rich. Supplement with leaf mold. Acid to alkaline 5.5–7.5 pH.
Shade degree: Partial shade.
Watering requirement: Water regularly.
Spacing of plants: 10 in. (25 cm) apart.
Tips and care: Works well along rock walls and rock gardens.

Common name: Wintergreen
Scientific name: *Gaultheria procumbens*
Description: Aromatic evergreen ground cover with tiny, bell-shaped white flowers tinged with pink followed by bright-red, mint-flavored berries grows to 6 in. (15 cm) tall. Leaves, which are thick and leathery, 1–2 in. (25–50 mm) long, grow off woody stalks and turn bronze in autumn.
Plant hardiness: Zones 5–8.
Soil needs: Moist, well-drained, humus-rich soil. Fertility: moderately rich. Quite acid 4.0–6.0 pH.
Shade degree: Partial to full shade.
Watering requirement: Water regularly.
Spacing of plants: 1–2 ft. (30–60 cm) apart.
Tips and care: Grow from nursery starts rooted in sod. Brew dried leaves.

Common name: Yew, English
Scientific name: *Taxus baccata*
Description: Low-growing, mounded ground cover with ½-in. (13-mm) red berries (one male and one female plant are needed for cross-pollination) grows to 2 ft. (60 cm) tall and 6 ft. (1.8 m) wide. Needles are slightly curved and dark green with pale green stripes at the bottom.
Plant hardiness: Zones 6–8.
Soil needs: Moist, well-drained soil. Fertility: rich. Supplement with peat moss or leaf mold. Neutral 7.0 pH.
Shade degree: Partial to full shade.
Watering requirement: Keep soil moist. Tolerates moderate to dry soil.
Spacing of plants: 3–4 ft. (.9–1.2 m) apart.
Tips and care: Prune and shear any time to shape and keep compact.

Warning

The leaves, bark, and fruit of English Yew are toxic if ingested. Avoid planting in areas frequented by children or pets.

I thank you for the seeds... Too old to plant trees for my own gratification, I shall do it for my posterity.

THOMAS JEFFERSON

TREES

Common name: Dogwood, Flowering
Scientific name: *Cornus florida*
Description: Small bushy tree with 3–4-in-(8–10-cm) white or pink flowers followed by scarlet berries grows 20–35 ft. (6–10 m) tall. Leaves are oval, 3–6 in. (8–15 cm) long, and turn a deep red in autumn.
Plant hardiness: Zones 5–9.
Soil needs: Moist, well-drained soil. Fertility: rich. Acid 6.5 pH.
Shade degree: Light to partial shade.
Watering requirement: Water regularly, especially in summer; not drought tolerant.
Spacing of plants: 20–35 ft. (6–10 m) apart.
Tips and care: Works well as a framing tree. Not pollution tolerant. Susceptible to insects and disease.

Common name: Magnolia, Star

Scientific name: *Magnolia stellata*

Description: Slow-growing, many-branched tree with fragrant, star-shaped, white, 3–4-in.-wide (8–10-cm) flowers grows 6–15 ft. (1.8–4.5 m) tall. Leaves are oval, dark green, 4–5 in. (10–13 cm) long, and turn a yellow-bronze tinged with rose in autumn.

Plant hardiness: Zones 5–9.

Soil needs: Fertile, moist, well-drained soil. Fertility: rich. Supplement with peat moss or compost. Quite acid 5.5–6.5 pH.

Shade degree: Light to partial shade.

Spacing of plants: 6–15 ft. (1.8–4.5 m) apart.

Watering requirement: Water moderately.

Tips and care: Plant in protected area; if flower petals get frosted they will turn brown. Tolerant of urban pollution. Train to desired shape while plant is young.

Common name: Maple, Fullmoon

Scientific name: *Acer japonicum*

Description: Dainty, slow-growing tree grows 15–20 ft. (4.5–6 m) tall. Leaves are roundish, smooth, finely cut, and light green turning to ruby red in autumn.

Plant hardiness: Zones 5–9.

Soil needs: Moist, fertile soil. Fertility: rich. Supplemented with peat moss or leaf mold. Acid 6.5 pH.

Shade degree: Partial shade.

Watering requirement: Water moderately, well during dry spells.

Spacing of plants: 15–20 ft. (4.5–6 m) apart.

Tips and care: Tolerant of air pollution. Requires only a light pruning to shape.

Common name: Redbud, Eastern

Scientific name: *Cercis canadensis*

Description: Rounded tree with ½-in. (13-mm) purple-pink flowers (does not flower for 4–5 years after planting) grows 25–35 ft. (7.5–10.5 m) tall. Leaves are glossy, heart-shaped, and turn yellow in autumn.

Plant hardiness: Zones 4–9.

Soil needs: Deep, moist, well-drained soil. Fertility: average. No fertilization needed. Acid to alkaline 6.5–7.5 pH.

Shade degree: Open to partial shade; partial shade in late winter and spring stimulates the fullest flowering.

Watering requirement: Water regularly.

Spacing of plants: 25–35 ft. (7.5–10.5 m) apart.

Tips and care: Little care is needed once established. Buy young trees at less than 6 ft. (1.8 m) tall. Nice accent tree to dogwoods.

Common name: Silver Bell Tree

Scientific name: *Halesia carolina*

Description: Ornamental tree with white bell-shaped flowers grows 15–30 ft. (5–9 m) tall and 15–20 ft. (4.5–6 m) wide. Leaves are 2–4 in. (5–10 cm) long and turn yellow in autumn.

Plant hardiness: Zones 4–8.

Soil needs: Moist, well-drained soil. Fertility: rich. Supplement with peat moss or leaf mold. Acid 5.0–6.0 pH.

Shade degree: Light to partial shade.

Watering requirement: Water moderately.

Spacing of plants: 15–20 ft. (4.5–6 m) apart.

Tips and care: Very attractive next to evergreens and near azaleas or rhododendrons. Leaves are very pest resistant. Does not require pruning.

FERNS

Perhaps the most unsung but most indispensable plant in the shade garden is the fern. Ferns usually are the spear carriers, hanging about mid- to back-border, providing a backdrop for flowering shade plants. Seasoned shade gardeners understand well the true versatility of this plant.

Ferns come in a fascinating variety of leaf types, colors, and sizes, from tiny "button" ferns that grow in fissures to ferns that grow as tall as trees. Colors range from the silver green of the Japanese painted fern to the dark forest green of the Christmas fern to the lime green of the hay-scented fern to the blue-green of the marginal shield fern. There are ferns that prefer alkaline soil, such as the sleek-bladed hart's tongue and frothy maidenhair fern, and those that crave acid soil, such as the Korean tassel fern. Some, such as autumn fern and tassel fern, adapt well to dry shade. Many more, including Japanese painted fern and glade fern, grow well in moist shade. Still others, such as log fern, royal fern, and netted chain fern, prefer wet shade. All do best in dappled shade and loose soil.

Ferns are easy to plant [see Planting Ferns, pg. 50] and easy to maintain. They rarely need fertilizing, spread rapidly, and count among their array specimens that grow between 6 inches (15 cm) and 4 feet (120 cm) tall.

As a decorating element, ferns add a touch of grace and lightness to any planting area. Their signature fronds can be straplike to positively frilly—indeed, it's the interplay of various frond styles that often creates interest in shade borders. With a legacy of primeval history, ferns are in their element when surrounded by mosses, fallen logs, and rock walls. While ferns make splendid foils for smooth-flowered impatiens and other simple-leafed border plants, consider bringing them to the fore by planting a fern-only shade garden for a truly dramatic look.

FERNS

Common name: Lady Fern
Scientific name: *Athyrium filix-femina*
Description: Lacy, light-green, fine-cut fronds that turn yellow by late summer on stout and scaly stems, grows 2–3 ft. (60–90 cm) tall and 15 in. (38 cm) wide.
Plant hardiness: Zones 3–8.
Soil needs: Moist, well-drained soil. Fertility: rich. Supplement with organic matter. Acid to alkaline 6.5–7.5 pH.
Watering requirement: Water regularly, but do not allow soil to become soggy. Not drought tolerant.
Spacing of plants: 1–2 ft. (30–60 cm) apart.
Tips and care: Common to eastern U.S. Works well in borders and rock gardens; naturalizes in wildflower gardens.

Common name: Maidenhair Fern, Northern
Scientific name: *Adiantum pedatum*
Description: Arching, light-green, lacy fronds on black stems grows 1–2 ft. (30–60 cm) tall.
Plant hardiness: Zones 3–8.
Soil needs: Moist, even boggy soil. Fertility: rich. Neutral 7.0 pH.
Shade degree: Light to moderate shade.
Watering requirement: Water regularly; do not let soil dry out. Not drought tolerant
Spacing of plants: 12–18 in. (30–45 cm) apart.
Tips and care: Nice in rock or woodland gardens, against walls or foundations. Watch out for slugs.

Common name: Ostrich Fern
Scientific name: *Matteuccia struthiopteris*
Description: Bright-green whorled fronds with big feathery plumes and lance-shaped leaflets; deciduous fern grows 4 ft. (1.2 m) tall and 2 ft. (60 cm) wide.
Plant hardiness: Zones 3–8.
Soil needs: Moist, well-drained soil. Fertility: average. Acid to neutral 6.5–7.0 pH.
Shade degree: Light shade.
Watering requirement: Water regularly; do not allow soil to dry out.
Spacing of plants: 2 ft. (60 cm) apart.
Tips and care: Presents a formal appearance perfect for moist borders and rock walls. Naturalizes near streams or ponds.

Common name: Royal Fern
Scientific name: *Osmunda regalis*
Description: Clump-forming 4-in. (10-cm) rich-green leaflets that turn bright yellow in autumn; deciduous fern grows 4–6 ft. (1.2–1.8 m) tall.
Plant hardiness: Zones 2–10.
Soil needs: Moist, or even boggy, well-drained soil. Fertility: rich. Supplement with organic matter. Acid 5.5–6.5 pH.
Shade degree: Light shade.
Watering requirement: Water regularly.
Spacing of plants: 3 ft. (90 cm) apart.
Tips and care: Excellent to screen walls or other structures. Nice planted with shrubs. Works well in moist banks or along streams. One of the tallest of ferns; lends dramatic form and texture to the garden.

> *All gardens are a form of autobiography.*
> ROBERT DASH

BULBS

Common name: Caladium
Scientific name: *Caladium*
Description: Stemless tropical bulb with insignificant flowers grows to 18 in. (45 cm) tall. Leaves are large, heart- or arrow-shaped in combinations of light green, white, pink, or red, sometimes all on one leaf.
Plant hardiness: Zones 9–11.
Soil needs: Moist, well-drained soil. Fertility: rich. Neutral 7.0 pH.
Shade degree: Light to full shade.
Watering requirement: Water regularly.
Spacing of plants: 12 in. (30 cm) apart and 1–3 in. (25–75 mm) deep.
Tips and care: Native to South America. Very attractive planted next to summer flowers in borders and containers and in any ornamental planting. Protect from wind. When leaves die, allow soil to dry out and the plant will ripen. Store tubers in a cool place throughout winter.

Common name: Crocus, Autumn
Scientific name: *Crocus longiflorus*
Description: Low-growing bulbs with 3–5½-in.-wide (8–14-cm), lilac-purple flowers that have a yellow throat grows 5 in. (13 cm) tall. Leaves are glossy.
Plant hardiness: Zones 5–10.
Soil needs: Moist, humus- rich, well-drained soil. Fertility: moderately rich to rich. Neutral 7.0 pH.
Shade degree: Light shade.
Watering requirement: Water moderately.
Spacing of plants: 4–6 in. (10–15 cm) apart and 3 in. (8 cm) deep.
Tips and care: Works well along a lawn or in rock gardens.

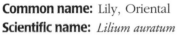

Common name: Lily, Oriental
Scientific name: *Lilium auratum*
Description: Fragrant bulb with 8–10-in.-wide (20–25-cm) white, cherry-red, or other-colored flowers stippled with darker markings grows 6 ft. (1.8 m) tall or more.
Plant hardiness: Zones 4-8.
Soil needs: Moist, well-drained soil. Fertility: rich. Acid to neutral 6.5–7.0 pH.
Shade degree: Partial shade.
Watering requirement: Water regularly.
Spacing of plants: 2 ft. (60 cm) apart and 4 in. (10 cm) deep.
Tips and care: Good for borders and containers and against walls or fences.

Common name: Orchid
Scientific name: *Orchidacae*
Description: 1-in.–50-ft.-long (25 mm–150-m) stalks with tiny–foot-wide (30-cm) three-petaled yellow, mauve, pink, white, rose, brown, orange, purple, green, or scarlet flowers. Leaves generally are a light grass-green, but many different varieties sport unusual foliage.
Plant hardiness: Zones 3–10.
Soil needs: Orchid soils come packaged. Fertilize with water-soluble fertilizer every 2 weeks.
Shade degree: Partial shade.
Water requirement: Water regularly, at least once a week during the growth period, then allow the soil to dry out between waterings.
Spacing of plants: 6-in. (3-cm) pot when planting reaches flowering age (18 months).
Tips and care: Maintain 65–70 percent humidity by misting.

U.S.D.A. Plant Hardiness Zones
of North America

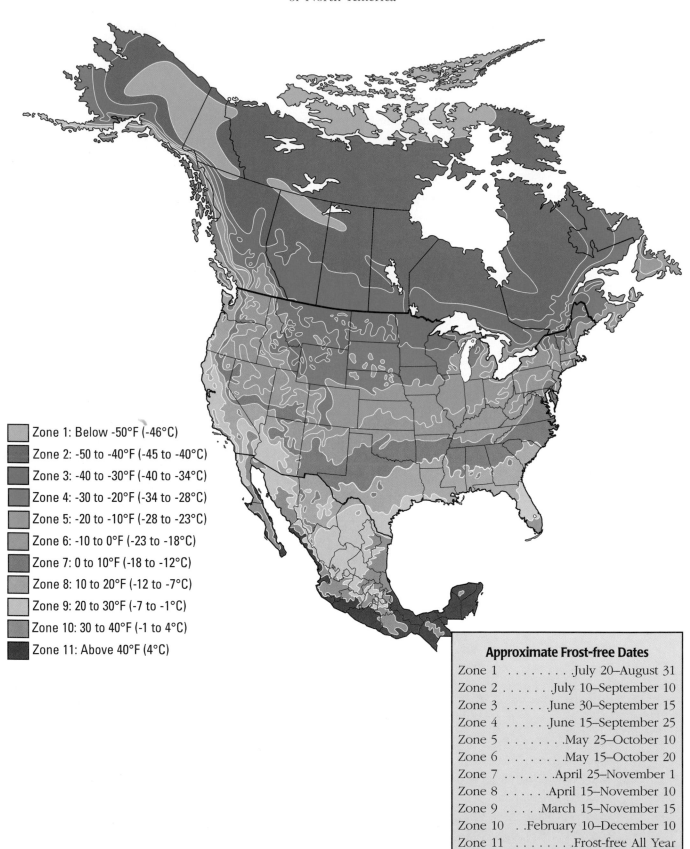

Zone 1: Below -50°F (-46°C)

Zone 2: -50 to -40°F (-45 to -40°C)

Zone 3: -40 to -30°F (-40 to -34°C)

Zone 4: -30 to -20°F (-34 to -28°C)

Zone 5: -20 to -10°F (-28 to -23°C)

Zone 6: -10 to 0°F (-23 to -18°C)

Zone 7: 0 to 10°F (-18 to -12°C)

Zone 8: 10 to 20°F (-12 to -7°C)

Zone 9: 20 to 30°F (-7 to -1°C)

Zone 10: 30 to 40°F (-1 to 4°C)

Zone 11: Above 40°F (4°C)

Approximate Frost-free Dates

Zone 1 . . . . July 20–August 31

Zone 2 . . . . . . July 10–September 10

Zone 3 . . . . . June 30–September 15

Zone 4 . . . . . June 15–September 25

Zone 5 . . . . .May 25–October 10

Zone 6 . . . . .May 15–October 20

Zone 7 . . . . . . .April 25–November 1

Zone 8 . . . . . .April 15–November 10

Zone 9 . . . . .March 15–November 15

Zone 10 . .February 10–December 10

Zone 11 . . . . .Frost-free All Year

T

The United States Department of Agriculture (USDA) Plant Hardiness Zone Map provides a general guide to growing conditions in North America. It divides the continent into 11 zones based on the average minimum annual temperatures within each zone. The zones roughly predict which plants will survive in a given area. Because weather varies from year to year, the actual minimum temperatures may be lower or higher than indicated on the plant hardiness map.

Find your locale on the map, then identify your zone by comparing its color to the legend. Many growers include zone adaptation information on their plant tags and seed packages for your convenience.

Remember, true annual plants are genetically programmed to live for no more than a year, regardless of where they're planted, so hardiness zones mainly affect them by limiting the length of the garden season. Perennials, biennials, shrubs, and trees, on the other hand, grow only in zones where they've adapted to the climate.

When you're planting a shade garden, use the information contained in the map to guide your plant selections. Your major concern other than plant hardiness zone will be the first and last frost dates in your area [see chart, opposite]. Sow seed indoors for cold-season plants—those that tolerate soil temperatures for germination of 40–50°F (4–10°C)—six weeks before the last frost. Wait a few more weeks for warm-season plants—those that prefer planting temperatures of 60°F (16°C) or higher. The average first and last frost dates for your area are general guidelines, however, not guarantees.

Moreover, zone maps and frost charts alike can't account for the effects of thermal belts, nearby bodies of water, and other factors that create microclimates within zones Only careful observation will give you an accurate picture of climatic conditions in your own backyard.

Climate and microclimate govern plant choices and when gardens are planned and planted

Plant Hardiness

Find your plant hardiness zone on the U.S.D.A. scale by identifying your locale, noting its color, and comparing that color to the legend. Remember that local conditions— shade, slope of site, prevailing winds, or other factors—may cause your garden to vary from the surrounding area by a zone or more.

ON-LINE INDEX

INDEX

INDEX